# Starting out
## with your
## laptop

Copyright - Editions ENI - July 2004

ISBN: 2-7460-2402-0
Original edition: ISBN: 2-7460-2280-X

## Editions ENI
BP 32125
44021 NANTES Cedex 1
Tel: 33.(0)2.51.80.15.15
Fax: 33.(0)2.51.80.15.16

e-mail: editions@ediENI.com
http://www.editions-eni.com

**WAY IN** collection directed by Corinne Hervo

## Foreword

This book has been written for beginners who want to know how to get the most from their laptop computer using Windows XP and the different features that their Windows applications offer.

You can consult the different parts of this book separately but they have been designed to be taken in order. This way, you will first discover the different hardware components of your portable computer and how they fit together. When you have connected everything up, the second part of this book will show you how to start your computer and work comfortably in the Windows environment. The third part deals with three applications that many computers offer: the Word word processor, and the Works integrated software package. You can use these applications to create documents and save them on your hard disk, while the fourth part describes how you can use the Windows Explorer to manage your documents. If you have an Internet connection you can take your first trip on this "information highway" using the fifth part of this book as your guide. The sixth part describes typical problems you may encounter together with the messages that will appear on your screen in such situations: this final part will prepare you to deal with such problems, if and when they occur.

This book is not just for reading; it is essentially to be put into practice. Sit down at your computer and try out the actions described by following the examples. Keep this book close to your computer and you will find it a useful reference for finding a function or term that you may have forgotten.

Not only will you find information on the features that Windows offers, you will also find tips on what not to do and what not to forget, as well as convenient shortcuts to help you save time. You can often carry out the same action using the mouse, the keyboard or the menus. These symbols will help you between each type of

method: ⌨ for a keyboard method, 🖱 for a method that uses the mouse and ☰ for the method using the menus. You may also come across the following symbols:

🗝 indicates a comment with extra information about the current topic.

💡 indicates a useful tip.

**The only way to learn about your computer is to use it: settle down in front of your screen, prop this book up next to the keyboard... and you will soon see that your computer is not as complicated as you might have thought.**

# Table ────────────────
## of contents

## Getting to know the hardware — **1st Part**

### Describing the portable computer — Chapter 1.1

| | |
|---|---|
| The portable computer | 12 |
| Power supply and plugs | 13 |
| Main unit features | 13 |

### How your computer works — Chapter 1.2

| | |
|---|---|
| The main unit | 20 |
| The processor | 21 |
| The hard disk | 22 |
| The memory | 23 |
| The floppy disk drive | 24 |
| The CD-ROM/DVD drive/writer | 25 |
| The keyboard | 26 |
| The mouse | 31 |

### Other external devices — Chapter 1.3

| | |
|---|---|
| Printers | 34 |
| Modem | 36 |
| Zip drive | 37 |
| Scanners | 38 |
| Digital cameras | 39 |
| Joysticks | 40 |

# Table
## of contents

USB flash drives                                               41

PCMCIA cards or PC-cards                                        41

## Discovering the environment                    2nd Part

### The desktop                                   Chapter 2.1

Starting Windows XP                                            44

Discovering the Windows XP desktop                             46

Start menu                                                     47

Closing a Windows XP session (logging off)                     49

Switching off your computer                                    50

### Basic operations                              Chapter 2.2

Starting an application from the start menu                    52

General window items                                           53

Moving and resizing a window                                   54

Managing several windows                                       55

Managing an application's menus and options                    58

Filling in dialog boxes                                        60

Leaving an application (closing a window)                      61

# Table
## of contents

## Getting to know Word and Works     3rd Part

### Word: a word processor     Chapter 3.1

| | |
|---|---:|
| Starting Microsoft Word | 64 |
| Getting started with the workscreen | 65 |
| Entering text | 67 |
| Using insert/overtype mode | 69 |
| Inserting a tab | 69 |
| Deleting text | 71 |
| Moving the insertion point | 71 |
| Selecting text | 72 |
| Moving/copying text | 74 |
| Saving a new document | 74 |
| Opening a document | 76 |
| Saving an existing document | 77 |
| Closing a document | 77 |
| Formatting characters | 78 |
| Changing text alignment in paragraphs | 81 |
| Starting the print preview | 82 |
| Printing a document | 83 |
| Printing part of a document | 83 |

# Table
# of contents

## Works: a software suite

Starting Microsoft Works   86

Using the Task Launcher   88

Creating a document   90

Description of the spreadsheet window   91

Moving around a spreadsheet   92

Entering data   93

Editing the contents of a cell   94

Deleting the contents of a cell   95

Entering a calculation formula   95

Inserting a function into a formula   96

Copying the contents of a cell to adjacent cells   97

Inserting rows/columns   98

Deleting rows/columns   99

Changing column widths   99

Changing row heights   100

Formatting characters   101

Saving, opening and closing a Works document   103

Using the Print preview   103

Printing a document   104

Closing Works applications   106

# Table
## of contents

## Windows XP                                    **4th Part**

### My Documents window                          Chapter 4.1

Discovering the My Documents window                    108

Displaying an Explorer bar in a folder window          109

Accessing a drive or a folder                          110

Changing the presentation of the folder/file list     113


### Managing folders and files                   Chapter 4.2

Creating a folder                                      116

Selecting folders and files                            118

Searching for files according to their names           119

Moving folders and files                               122

Copying folders and files                              123

Copying folders or files to a floppy disk              124

Deleting folders and files                             124

Managing folders and files in the Recycle Bin          126

Formatting a floppy disk                               127


### Installing                                   Chapter 4.3

Installing a printer                                   130

Installing an external screen                          133

Installing a program (application)                     134

Uninstalling a program (application)                   136

# Table ──────────
## of contents

**The Briefcase**          Chapter 4.4

What is the Briefcase used for?        138

Using the Briefcase        138

## Multimedia and communication      **5th Part**

**Windows Media Player**        Chapter 5.1

Discovering the Windows Media Player        144

Playing an audio CD        145

Listening to the radio        147

Media Player and DVDs        150

Changing the look of the Windows Media Player        152

**Getting started on the Internet**        Chapter 5.2

Accessing the Internet        154

The different steps to connection        154

Understanding the different uses of the Internet        157

**Working with the browser**        Chapter 5.3

Understanding the Web and the role of browsers        158

Starting your browser        158

Displaying your first Web page        159

Activating hyperlinks in a page        160

# Table

## of contents

**E-mail**                                                                 Chapter 5.4

E-mail addresses                                                                    162

Getting to know your e-mail software                                                163

Sending a message                                                                   163

Collecting your mail                                                                165

Attached files (attachments)                                                        166


## Troubleshooting                                                          6th Part

**Technical problems**                                                     Chapter 6.1

Floppy disk                                                                         168

Drive inaccessible                                                                  168

System error                                                                        169

File errors                                                                         169

Close window                                                                        169

Office application message                                                          170

Hardware problem                                                                    171

Printer problem                                                                     171

Internet errors                                                                     171


**Index**                                                                           173

## Introduction

Computing is becoming increasingly important for all of us, young or old. In fact, computers are involved in some form in practically everything we do today and who can guess what computing's role might be tomorrow?

Charles Babbage designed the first general purpose computer in England in 1833. This so-called Analytical Engine followed instructions from punched cards. In the next century, electronics were used to dramatic effect. An early example of an electronic computer was the ENIAC. Built in the United States in 1946 out of 17,468 electronic vacuum tubes, the ENIAC weighed 30 tonnes and covered 72 square metres!

The miniaturisation of electronic components led to a veritable revolution in the computing world. A key event in this progression was the invention of the microprocessor by Intel in 1971: in comparison to the ENIAC, the Intel 4004 weighed a few grams, was 4.2 cm long and 3.2 cm wide! Since that date, the microprocessor, the central computing element, has undergone numerous developments leading to the rapid expansion of computing in the 1980's.

During this period, two great computing hardware families came to the fore: Apple and IBM.

The Apple computer, later to become the Macintosh, was the only one to offer a graphical environment with icons and the use of a mouse: this was the first version of the interface that all micro-computers provide today. Today, graphics and multimedia professionals frequently use Apple equipment.

For their part, IBM launched a new type of computing hardware, called the PC or Personal Computer. Up until this time, only large industries used computing, in the form of computers wired up to huge "cabinets" that stored all the information. The PC offered computing for all: used at first in the workplace, the PC later came into the home. Several companies developed this new market, offering IBM-compatible PCs.

Micro-computers at that time used 8086 microprocessors and ran in the MS-DOS interface: this consisted of a black screen on which you wrote specific words and phrases, similar to those of a programming language.

From this time, processing capacity on average has doubled every year. The 8086 gave way to the 286 (with over three times as much processing power) which in turn was superseded by the 386 and then by the 486 (which was four times faster than the 386). Several versions of this processor appeared, with higher and higher processing speeds, which are measured in MHz: the first 486 ran at 25 MHz, while the final 486 processed at 100 MHz. In 1993, Intel brought out a new processor, called the Pentium, which was able to transmit data twice as fast as any of its predecessors. Intel has since brought out the Pentium 2, Pentium 3, Celeron and Pentium 4 processors.

# Introduction

As the need grew for certain users to be able to move around with their computers, manufacturers began to create portable computers. Early models were more "transportable" than "portable", but the miniaturization of electronic components, the advent of flat screens and other innovations has led to the development of computers the size of a piece of paper and a few centimeters thick, which give a more accurate meaning to the term "laptop" computer.

In parallel with these hardware developments, the software has been changing too. The text-mode environment on MS-DOS gave way to the graphical Windows environment: Windows has opened the floodgates to multimedia (sound, pictures and video) and to the Internet, transforming the computer into an indispensable and fascinating tool.

# 1st

*Now that you have bought your laptop and brought it home, you are no doubt eager to start working with it. This section will lead you through a description of the various features and add-ons that your computer offers and explains what purpose they serve.*

# Part

## Getting to know the hardware

**1.1 Describing the portable computer**   p.12

**1.2 How your computer works**   p.20

**1.3 Other external devices**   p.34

# Describing the portable computer

These days, hardware changes so fast that a computer is up to date for only a short period of time. One model may be replaced by the next in the space of a few weeks!

Since they first appeared, personal computers, and in particular portable computers (often called "laptops" or "notebooks"), have come a long way. The first "portable" computers were as big as sewing machine; the screen had a cathode ray tube and the whole thing weighed up to 15 kilos! Today's laptops weigh often less than a kilo.

## THE PORTABLE COMPUTER

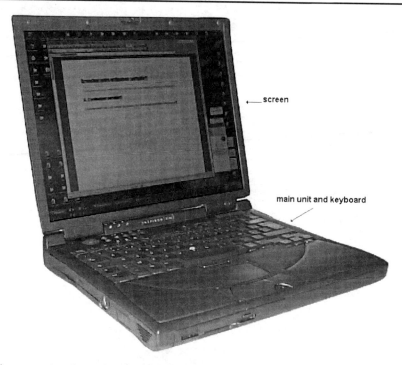

← screen

main unit and keyboard

The computer shown here is made by a well-known brand and has practically all the options you could hope for on this type of equipment. Unlike desktop computers, you cannot usually upgrade a laptop's different parts.

Some manufacturers will offer certain fixed, predefined configurations. Others offer an array of features and will construct the laptop to your specifications.

While this may be the case, remember that once you have unwrapped your longed-for laptop, you will not have much leeway for improving it. On most portable computers, you can add memory, on some you can change the hard disk, but generally speaking, the possibilities stop there.

One advantage that your laptop will have is a variety of plugs and ports so you can attach it to a large range of devices.

 A device is an external piece of equipment that you plug in to your computer and which offers features that the computer itself cannot provide. Common devices include a printer, a scanner, a modem, a mouse, a keyboard, a joystick and so on.

## POWER SUPPLY AND PLUGS

- Often to use your laptop, you will not even need to plug it in. As it works by battery, simply open it up and press the on/off button.

- If you have just bought the computer, it is likely that the battery won't be charged. A mains power adaptor will be provided with the machine, and you should use this when you are not on the move and for intensive use. This spares you from seeing the computer suddenly switch off because the battery has run down (which can prove somewhat alarming!).

## MAIN UNIT FEATURES

- The main unit is the heart of any computer. All the useful items are enclosed in this box, which, in the case of a laptop, also contains the keyboard.

- We can now take a close look at what this main unit contains. While the pictures in this book are only an example of a particular brand of computer and may not look exactly like your own, remember that most of what it contains will vary only slightly and the various plugs and switches will be more or less the same. The items that follow are no doubt on your laptop, even if they are not in exactly the same place!

## Seen from above

- on/off button
- audio buttons
- keyboard
- track point
- touch pad
- wrist-rest

If you look at it from above, you can see the following items on the main unit (from top to bottom):

The **on/off button** switches the machine on. How you turn it off depends on how shutdown has been programmed in Windows. Most of the time, you will not need to use it to turn off the computer, as you can stop it by using one of the options in the **start** menu, as you will see in the next chapter.

The **audio buttons** differ largely from one computer to the next and sometimes there are none. You use them to control the sound volume and sometimes to manage playing audio CDs.

The **keyboard** is a scaled-down version of the one usually found on desktop computers. You can see that the number pad on the right (that shows numbers 0 to 9 and mathematical symbols) is missing. The keyboard is described in detail further on in this chapter.

The **track point** is a kind of miniature joystick that you push with your finger and which moves the pointer on the screen. This mouse-replacement device is not supplied with all laptops.

The **touch pad** is a lightly-coated square of plastic on which you move your finger to move the pointer on the screen. It does the same job as the track point described above.

The **wrist-rests** are not always as well-defined as in this picture; this empty space in front of the keyboard is for you to rest your wrists on as you type, to prevent fatigue.

## Seen face on

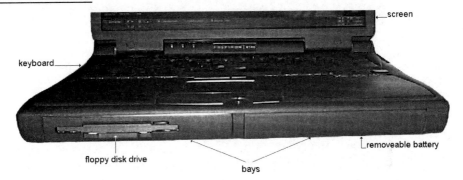

screen

keyboard

floppy disk drive

bays

removeable battery

- A portable computer sometimes gives you the chance to remove some of the drives, like the floppy disk or CD-ROM drive and also the battery. The areas used for this are called **bays**. On the photo above, you can see two bays, one for the floppy drive and a second for the battery.

- A floppy disk is a magnetic disk in a slim plastic case. You can use them to store documents, photos, and other files that you work with on your computer. Floppy disks are described in the section dealing with how your computer works.

### Seen from the left side

On the left side of the laptop, you can see (from left to right):

CD-Rom/DVD drive     S-video jack     speaker

The **CD-ROM** and/or **DVD drive**. There is a button (here the oval button that the arrow points to) which you press to open the drive.

The **S-video jack** lets you plug your computer into a television, on which you can view DVDs or picture slide shows. This connection is not available on all laptops, although it is more and more common. If there is a jack, the manufacturer will no doubt have supplied an adapter cable with the computer that you can plug into this jack to convert it to a standard video outlet.

Here is an example of a video cable (this was supplied with the computer shown):

The **speaker**, and there will be a second one on the opposite side, provides stereo sound.

## Seen from the right side

There is not much elbow room on this side! From left to right you can see:

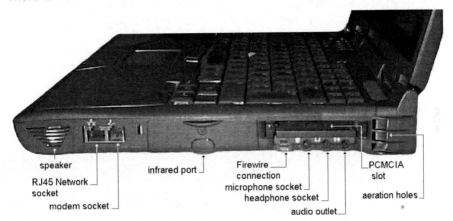

speaker     infrared port    Firewire     PCMCIA
RJ45 Network     connection     slot
socket     microphone socket
modem socket     headphone socket    aeration holes
audio outlet

The second stereo sound **speaker**.

The **network socket** (also called RJ45). Here you can plug in a network cable to connect your laptop to a local network and communicate with the other computers and servers on that network.

The **modem socket** receives a modem cable so you can plug the computer into a telephone outlet and send and receive faxes and connect to the Internet.

The **infrared communication port** (also called IrDA) is an inlaid red plastic window, behind which there are infrared LEDs (lamps), like on a television remote control. Thanks to this wireless feature, various devices can exchange data with the computer, such as printers, handhelds, mobile phones and so on.

The **Firewire socket** (also called IEEE 1394) accepts a special cable for high-speed data exchange with certain devices (but apart from digital cameras, few devices currently use this type of plug).

The **microphone socket** is used to plug in a standard microphone to record sounds and voice. Most laptops also have an in-built microphone in the main unit, near the keyboard.

The **headphone socket** takes any personal stereo type of headphone. This is also the sound outlet that you will plug into your television if you use the video outlet to watch DVDs.

# Describing the portable computer

The **audio outlet** can be used to plug in an audio device such as a stereo, so you could record from an audio CD or cassette onto the hard disk.

The **PCMCIA slot** (or PC card) accepts PCMCIA cards. These cards, about the size of a credit card, are used for various purposes. There are modem or network cards, external hard disks and so on, that use this connection format. Nevertheless, most devices currently use USB connections. The USB plugs are described with the items seen at the back of the computer.

### Seen from behind

The back of the computer also contains a large number of sockets and ports (from left to right):

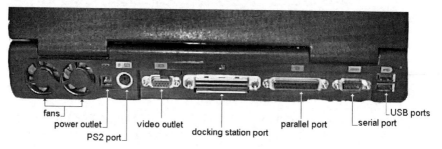

fans
power outlet
PS2 port
video outlet
docking station port
parallel port
serial port
USB ports

The **fans** come on automatically once the computer reaches a certain temperature, to cool it off. This happens without any intervention on your part, but you should take care that there is nothing blocking these holes.

The **power outlet** differs greatly from one brand to another. Use this to plug the laptop into the mains power, which is highly recommended if you work on the computer for a long period of time.

The **PS2 port** takes a standard mouse or keyboard. Many users find these more comfortable to use than the in-built keyboard or the touch pad and track point.

The **video outlet** is used to attach an external screen. Recent laptops generally manage two screens independently. This means you can display different applications simultaneously to get the most out of your computer's features.

Getting to know the hardware

18

The **docking station port** is specific to each brand. This connection is used to attach the laptop to a docking station. A docking station is a platform of varying size that you attach to the laptop and which offers various sockets and connections that the laptop may not have. These stations are used less and less as the number of connections provided directly on the laptop increase. Also, USB ports are used more and more and eventually all devices will probably use that standard.

The **parallel port** is generally used to attach printers.

The **serial port** is not used so frequently these days. Some modems still use this type of connection. On the whole, most devices now use USB ports.

The **USB ports** offer a very versatile type of connection as you can plug different devices one into the other. USB ports also offer plug and play capabilities, which means you can plug (or unplug) devices as you work and the computer will recognize them, without you restarting the computer.

# How your computer works

*Now that you have seen how the portable computer looks from the outside, you can get an idea of what is inside it. The items described here are found in all computers, regardless of their make.*

## THE MAIN UNIT

As you saw in the previous chapter, a portable computer is made up of two parts, one being the screen and the other the main unit.

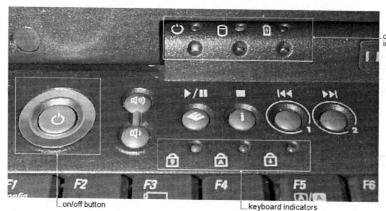

on/off and disk indicators

on/off button          keyboard indicators

The illustration above is an enlargement of the area that houses several buttons and indicators. Your computer may not have exactly the same ones, but they will be similar.

- The **on/offbutton** turns the computer on. Generally speaking you can turn off the computer from Windows using the **Shut Down** command in the **start** menu. This is explained in a later chapter. It is useful to know though that if your computer "crashes" (although the correct term is "hang", meaning that the keyboard and mouse no longer respond), you can turn it off by holding down the on/off button for about 4 or 5 seconds. In this situation it is often the only way to turn off the computer (aside from pulling out the plug...).

- The indicator lights on the photo (from left to right) are the power indicator, the disk activity indicator and the battery indicator. Refer to your computer's user manual to see exactly what these lights indicate.

## THE PROCESSOR

- The processor is the "brain" of your computer. It runs all the instructions that carry out the work you specify on the keyboard, from displaying a picture, to playing a DVD. The processor is closely linked to another component called a clock, which indicates how fast it runs in hertz. A hertz refers to a vibration or beat rate per second. As computer clocks are very fast, their speed is referred to in terms of megahertz (MHz), which means a million hertz or vibrations per second, or even gigahertz (GHz) for a billion hertz.

- Currently, clock (and consequently processor) speeds for high-performance personal computers are in the region of 3 GHz.

This is a processor from a normal desktop computer. The shape and size varies depending on the manufacturer and model.

# How your computer works

## THE HARD DISK

*This picture shows the inside of a standard hard disk; the disk in a laptop is much smaller than this.*

- The hard disk as a set of metal and magnetic disks enclosed in a plastic box. These disks contain the operating system of your computer (the program that makes all the rest work!). In general this is Windows, which is described in another chapter.

- The hard disk also contains the other applications (programs) that you install and all the data files that create with those programs. Your text documents, pictures or films are all stored on the hard disk.

- A hard disk's storage capacity is measured in bytes. A byte corresponds more or less to a character (letter, figure or symbol) and you can use this analogy to get an idea of what can fit on a disk. Processor speeds are increasing and so is the average capacity of a hard disk, which means that capacity is expressed in terms of megabytes (MB, a million bytes), gigabytes (GB, or a billion bytes) and even terabytes (TB, or a thousand gigabytes).

- On average, today's hard disks has capacities ranging from 40 to 120 GB. Some desktop computers have disks of up to 250 GB but portable computers rarely exceed 80 GB.

- This difference in capacity is explained by the fact that the hard disks in laptops are physically smaller than those in an ordinary computer.

While these figures were correct at the time of publication, standards are evolving so fast that they may be outdated by the time you read this!

## THE MEMORY

The photo above shows a SO-DIMM memory module, which is the type generally used in portable computers.

- A computer's memory is a set of electronic components that your computer uses to temporarily store information as you work. When you turn on the computer, the programs are loaded into the memory from the hard disk and from there the processor can make them work.

- When you use software and create files (text, pictures etc.) these are handled in the memory. Before you turn off the computer, you must save what you want to keep on the hard disk or it will be lost.

- The working memory described here is called the RAM (random access memory). Its capacity is measured in bytes, as for the hard disk, with the same variations (MB, GB etc.).

- The memory capacity of today's computers varies between 64 to 512 MB and upwards. Your memory needs depend on the applications you are going to use and the type of data you will be working with. You will need more memory if you will be working with images or videos than if you are going to be just writing text. Generally speaking, the higher your computer's RAM, the better it will perform (although this is not an exclusive criterion).

## THE FLOPPY DISK DRIVE

Lotus.  Disk 1 of 1
Instructor Data File
Lotus Domino 4.5 and Notes 4.5
Intro to LotusScript in Notes

© Copyright 1997 Lotus Development
Corporation. All rights reserved.

T02820

write-protect switch
(you cannot write to
the disk if the hole
is open)

put this side
in first

protective cover

- A floppy disk is another way of storing documents and files. A floppy is a magnetic disk encased in a slim plastic case (which is actually hard, although the old 5 inch types were reasonably flexible!).

- A floppy disk does not offer anywhere near the type of storage space available on other media. The photo above shows a standard floppy disk whose capacity is only 1.44 megabytes.

- For this reason (but also because they tend to be unreliable), floppy disks and the matching drive are becoming an extinct species. While you can still store several text or even spreadsheet documents on a floppy disk, it would be too small for pictures, let alone videos. It is being largely replaced by ZIP disks, re-writeable CD-ROMs (CD-RWs) and USB flash drives.

- The lightest laptops have no floppy disk drive and often no CD-ROM drive either. In this case, you would use an external drive that can be plugged into a specific socket or into a USB port.

The **ZIP disk** and the **USB flash drive** (also called **pen drive** or just **USB drive**) are looked on as external devices, as they are not in-built but have to be plugged into the computer. External devices are dealt with in a different chapter.

## THE CD-ROM/DVD DRIVE/WRITER

▨ As described above, budget-priced laptops, or those that are super-light, often have no CD-ROM drive. Models that do have this type of drive often offer a combined CD-ROM/DVD player and writer.

▨ A writer (or burner) is a CD-ROM drive on which you can also write (copy, burn) onto a disk. You can buy one of two types of blank CD for this:

- CD-R disks (CD-Recordable) can only be written on once; you cannot erase what is on them.
- CD-RW disks (CD-ReWriteable) can be recorded onto more than once. You can delete their contents and write on them again (in theory up to 1000 times).

▨ If you wish to write CD-ROMs, you need a special type of software (this is often provided with the computer). Windows XP (described in a later chapter) has an integrated CD-burning application.

▨ Modern drives often double as DVD drives. In this case, your computer will probably be provided with an application that can read DVDs.

# How your computer works

*A computer is a machine to which you give orders (open a menu, colour this text and so on) and into which you enter data (typing in the text of a letter, giving a file name to that letter etc.). To supply the computer with this data, you use the keyboard, which is a far cry from old typewriter keyboards.*

## THE KEYBOARD

- The keyboard on a portable computer is much smaller than that of a standard desktop computer, even though it does supply the same keys (and then some!).

- To get around the problem of space, some keys have several functions. This is already the case on any keyboard but on a laptop this is taken to the extreme. You can tell these added symbols as they are usually in a different colour.

- The "double-up" keys are mainly those from the number pad. This is the right hand part of standard keyboard which is cut off on a laptop. The missing keys are then added to another part of the alphanumerical keyboard as shown above.

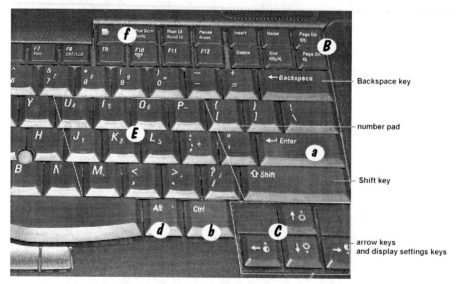

- If you want to use these keys, hold down a special key usually called **Fn** (for function) then, without letting go, press the required key.

▓ Some other keys also do two different jobs. For example, on the illustration above you can see that the four arrow keys in the bottom corner can also be used to adjust the screen's brightness and contrast (again in conjunction with the **Fn** key). Other "double" keys also exist at the top of the keyboard.

▓ What these keys do varies depending on the make and model of the portable computer. You will generally find keys for:

- adjusting the display,
- opening the CD-ROM/DVD drive,
- putting the computer on standby,
- adjusting the sound,
- changing screen,
- and so on.

The picture here shows the left side of the screen where the **Fn** key is located.

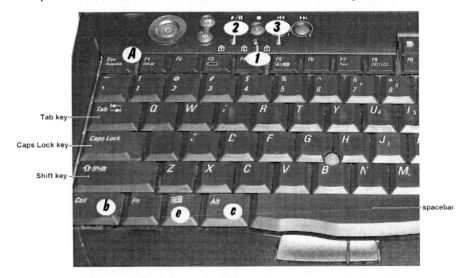

- The **Caps Lock** key locks the keyboard in capital letters mode. When you press this key, the Caps Lock indicator (1) comes on. If you then press a letter key, the letter will be in capitals. If you press a key with two or three characters (such as ⊞), the character at the top of the key will appear ($ in this example).

# How your computer works

- To turn off capitals, press the **Caps Lock** key again; the indicator light (1) goes out. Now when you press a letter key, the letter will be in lower case. If you press a key like ⬚ , the bottom character, in this case 5, will appear.
If you want to put only the first letter of a word in capitals, you do not need to use caps lock, just hold down the **Shift** key and at the same time press the required letter key. For multiple character keys, hold down the **Shift** key and press the ⬚ key to obtain the top character.
- The **Tab** key is used to position text with a specific alignment, predefined as a tab stop (cf. Word: a word processor - Inserting a tab).
- The **Backspace** key deletes the last characters you typed.
- The **Enter** key (a) is a vital key on the keyboard as it confirms all the information that you are sending to the computer. When you type text, you use it to create a new paragraph of text.

There are also a few special keys:

- The **Control** (b) and **Alt** (c) keys always work in combination with another key or with a click from the mouse. What they do depends on the application you are using.
- The **Alt Gr** key (d) is used to display the third character displayed on certain keys. For example, to produce a euro currency symbol, hold down the **Alt Gr** key and press the ⬚ key (**Control** plus **Alt** also performs the same function as **Alt Gr**).
- The **space bar** inserts a space in text (between two words for example).
- The **Windows** key (e) opens the Windows **start** menu.
- The **Menu** key (f) opens the shortcut menu, which is a menu of options that apply specifically to the item selected or pointed at.

Getting to know the hardware

28

The **function keys** (A) each perform a task, depending on the current application. Generally speaking you will find that the **F1** key always opens the application's help, which explains how to use the program.

The navigation keys (B) and the arrow keys (C), which you use to move to various items on the screen, can be seen at the extreme right of the keyboard.

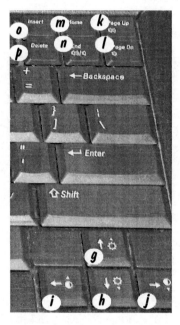

The first step to entering data is to tell the computer where that data must be added, for example in which paragraph of a document new text should be inserted. How the current data entry position appears on the screen varies according to the application, for example, in text it is represented by a flashing vertical line called the **insertion point**. The keys below move the insertion point within text:

- The **up arrow** (g) moves to the previous line of text.
- The **down arrow** (h) moves to the next line of text.
- The **left arrow** (i) moves on the same line, one character to the left.
- The **right arrow** (j) moves on the same line, one character to the right.

- The navigation keys (B) move the insertion point on a larger scale:
  - The **Page Up** key (k) goes to the previous screen page.
  - The **Page Down** key (l) goes to the next screen page.
  - The **Home** key (m) goes to the beginning of the line.
  - The **End** key (n) goes to the end of the line.
  - The **Insert** key (o) switches between overtype and insert mode. In insert mode, any new text is added to the existing text; in overtype mode, typing within existing text replaces the old text, character by character.
  - The **Delete** key (p) deletes characters to the right of the insertion point.
- On a portable computer, the number pad is built into the main keyboard:

The **Num Lock** key (a) turns the number lock on or off. When the number lock is on, the indicator (2) comes on. If you press a key from the number pad, the number appears, and not the letter that is also on the key. If you turn off the number lock, the keys behave as usual.

The number pad also contains keys for mathematical operations (+ for adding, - for subtracting , * for multiplying and / for dividing).

- Aside from the keys described above, there are also these special keys:

- The **Print Screen** key creates an image of the screen as it currently appears, which you can save or print.

- The **Scroll Lock** key was more widely-used with older applications in DOS, to allow scrolling of screen text up, down and sideways using the arrow keys. It is rarely used nowadays (although you can turn it on in Excel to scroll the spreadsheet with the arrow keys, but keeping the same cell active). When it is on, the indicator (3) lights up.
- The **Pause** key stops and restarts scrolling of a lot of information on the screen, only in certain applications. It is rarely used these days, although is still included in shortcut key combinations in some popular applications.
- The **Esc** key in the top left corner can often be used to cancel an action in progress, such as downloading a web page. It can often close a dialog box too.

 On some keyboards, you may find you need to press the **Shift** key to turn off **Caps Lock**.

*The mouse is now an indispensable tool in the Windows environment. If at first you may find it awkward to use, with practice you will work with it quite naturally.*
*Portable computers have replaced the traditional mouse with a touch pad or track point system. Although this is obviously useful for saving space, most people are more comfortable working with a real mouse. New types of wireless mouse are now available which are handy for laptops, as they take up little space and are more practical when you work for long periods.*

## THE MOUSE

Here is a small portable computer mouse, which has a two-way radio receiver that plugs into the computer's USB port.

**Getting to know the hardware**

- The mouse is used to interact with elements on the screen, such as opening a menu or selecting things. The current screen position of the mouse is symbolized by a white arrow called a **pointer** (although this symbol can change shape as you work in some applications). As you move the mouse on the mouse pad (or tabletop), you roll a ball underneath the mouse, which in turn instructs the pointer in which direction it should move.

- Once the pointer is pointing at the item on screen, click the mouse by pressing the left mouse button quickly then releasing it, to carry out the required action (open a menu, select an object etc.).

- Sometimes, you need to double-click to carry out an action. This means to make two clicks on the mouse button in rapid succession.

- If you need to select several items on screen, you may need to drag over them with the mouse. This means you place the pointer at the starting point, hold down the mouse button and as you hold it down, move the mouse in the required direction. When you are happy with the result (for example, when you have made your required selection), release the mouse button to confirm.

- There are two buttons on the mouse; the right mouse button can be used to right-click an item, which usually displays a shortcut menu with options specific to the pointed item.

- Some mice have a scroll wheel in between these two buttons, which you roll to move quickly in text. It performs the same action as the PgUp and PgDn keys.

 Some mice have three buttons. You can configure this kind of mouse so the middle button performs a certain task.

You should clean your mouse regularly. To do, turn the cover on top of the rubber ball to remove it, then take out the ball and gently rub any debris off the rollers that run against this ball. Use an implement that will not scratch the rollers, like a fingernail or toothpick, then blow out any dust or fluff inside the mouse.

You can now buy mice that do not work off a ball but through a laser detection system (optical mice). These require no maintenance and (theoretically) can run on uneven work surfaces.

# Other external devices

A device, or peripheral device, is any part of your computer that is not the CPU (Central Processing Unit) or the computer working memory. An external device is a device that is outside your main unit, such as your mouse or your keyboard. This section will describe some other external devices you can connect to your computer system. There are many different types of external device for varying needs, such as a printer to print your documents on paper, a modem to connect to the Internet, a CD-R drive or CD burner, a ZIP drive to backup your data, a scanner to enter your photos into your computer in the form of digital files, a digital camera, a joystick and so forth.

## PRINTERS

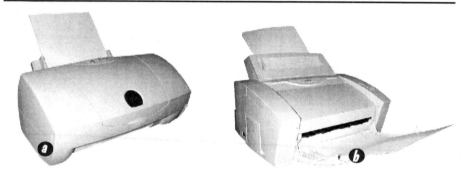

- Two types of printer are commonly used today: ink jet printers (a) and laser printers (b). Laser printers usually print black and white, as colour laser printers are quite expensive (approximately £ 1400 (€ 2 300), as opposed to £ 200 to £ 240 (€ 300 to 400) for a black and white model). Laser printers use toner cartridges (as with photocopy machines) and/or drums, according to the model and the make. Ink jet printers usually print colour and black and white. They use ink cartridges and most general purpose models are available in a price range from £ 50 to £ 130 (€ 75 to 220).

- A printer is supplied with:
  - toner or ink cartridges: you must change these regularly, which contributes to your running costs. The price of these consumable items varies according to the manufacturer.
  - a mains power cable (220 V).
  - a printer driver: a CD-ROM generally contains this item, which allows the operating system to recognise the printer. When you have connected up the printer you must install the printer software using this CD-ROM (cf. Installing - Installing a printer).

Getting to know the hardaware

The printer cable is generally not supplied with the printer. This cable links the printer to the computer main unit and carries information (data) between them. According to the type of printer cable you use, you connect the (c) end of this cable to the computer's parallel port (cf. Main unit) and the (d) end of this cable to the printer or the (e) end of the cable to the computer's USB port (cf. Main unit) and the (f) end of the cable to the printer.

Not all ink jet printers use the same type of colour cartridges: some ink jet printers use one black and white cartridge and one cartridge for each of the basic colours, while other ink jet printers use one black and white cartridge and one cartridge for all the colours. With the first approach, you need replace only the colour cartridge that has run out. With the second type, you must replace the complete, unique colour cartridge as soon as it runs out of one of its colours (the colour blue, for example).

When equipped with special photo paper and cartridges, some ink jet printers offer a print quality similar to that of photos.

# Other external devices

*With the continuing craze for the internet, you are probably eager to start surfing the Web. First, you must connect a modem between your main unit and your telephone socket.*

## MODEM

You can use a modem to send and receive data, on the Internet, but also for other items such as messages and faxes, across the telephone network.

▨ There are two types of modem:

- An internal modem resides as a board in the main unit. This type of modem works only when the computer is switched on.

- An external modem is housed in a separate casing that you can connect to any micro-computer. Most external modems operate even when your computer is switched off. This means that it can receive messages and faxes even when your computer is switched off. You can connect an external modem to your main unit, generally via a serial ports or one of the USB ports.

▨ An external modem is supplied with:

- a telephone cable,
- a manual,
- a serial cable (a) or USB cable (b).

*One of the golden rules of computing is to make at least one and possibly two backup copies of your important data. In this way, you can still work with your backup copy, even if you can no longer open a file (either because you overwrote or deleted it by accident) or for technical reasons (if the system can no longer find the file on your hard disk, for example). You can create backup copies in several ways. One of the simplest ways is to write your data to a ZIP disk.*

## ZIP DRIVE

▪ As with a floppy drive, the ZIP drive writes data to a removable storage medium. The main difference between these two types of disk is the capacity. The capacity of a floppy disk is only 1.44 MB (approximately one million characters, for example). A ZIP drive can store from 100 MB (the equivalent of 70 floppy disks) to 750 MB (520 floppies!), although the most common type is a 250 MB drive. A ZIP drive's capacity is usually part of its name, such as ZIP 750 MB.

▪ There are two types of ZIP drive, internal and external:

- An internal ZIP drive (a) usually appears directly under the floppy drive. In a laptop, the ZIP drive also acts as a floppy drive. ZIP drives are, however, relatively rare on a portable computer.

- an external ZIP drive (b) is contained in a separate casing that you can connect to your main unit via a parallel port (c) or a USB port (d): thus, you can install a ZIP drive on different computers with a minimum of fuss. The external ZIP drive is supplied with:

  - a cable to connect the drive to your computer (c) or (d),
  - a mains power cable,
  - a ZIP disk,

- an installation CD-ROM containing an application to use all the features of the ZIP drive.

*You can use the scanner to enter your photos into your computer in digital format, so that you can send them to your friends, or even modify the images.*

## SCANNERS

▨ A scanner scans a document such as a photo to capture its image and converts it to a digital file on your computer. You can then work on the file in an image-editing application like Photoshop or PaintShop Pro, save it as a file, print it (it can also be used as a photocopier) or fax it, if you have fax capabilities.

▨ The scanner is supplied with:

- a mains power cable (220 VAC),
- a cable to connect the device to your computer; this can be one of three types: parallel, USB or SCSI (pronounced "scuzzy").
- an installation CD-ROM containing the scanner driver that allows the operating system to recognise the scanner.
- image editing software.

Nowadays, some printers also act as scanners. However they accept only one-page documents. On the other hand, you can use a flat-bed scanner to scan from a book.

As the section above indicates, you can scan your photos into your computer. Alternatively, instead of taking a photo on paper, you can produce your photo directly with a digital camera in the form of a digital file, which you can then transfer onto your hard disk. This type of device is very useful as an independent means of producing your photos.

## DIGITAL CAMERAS

▨ You can use a digital camera to take photos that you can save on your computer to edit them or simply to print them, to send them to your friends by e-mail or to publish them on your personal web site.

▨ A digital camera is usually equipped with:

- a removal storage medium to store your pictures, such as a memory card. Memory cards have capacities ranging from 32 MB to 1 GB. How many photos you can store depends on the storage capacity of the card and on the resolution of the image (a low-resolution image may use a hundred kilobytes, a high-resolution one may use several megabytes!).

- a cable that you can connect to your computer via the USB connection, to transfer your pictures into your computer.

- a software application that allows you to view and edit these pictures.

▨ Digital cameras have similar features to traditional cameras, with:

- different lenses (36 mm, 140 mm and so forth),

- exposure control (shutter aperture and speed etc.),

- flash features (red eye reduction, automatic flash).

 Most digital cameras provide a small LCD screen for viewing your photo.

# Other external devices

*Joysticks are an alternative to the keyboard and are generally used to control arcade-type games such as racing circuits or flight simulators.*

## JOYSTICKS

- The joystick is an input device, as it transmits information to your computer's main unit.

- Joysticks are essentially used with video games. They replace the use of arrow keys and other keyboard shortcut keys. For example, the joystick provides a firing button, so you do not need to use the space key for this purpose, while another button provides a jump. However, it is not always easy to define these correspondences between the keyboard and the joystick.

- The joystick is supplied with:

  - a connection to the main unit (choose one with a USB connection so you will be sure of plugging it in),
  - a CD-ROM containing the installation software.

 Joysticks reduce keyboard wear and the damage that can occur when players are over-excited!

## USB FLASH DRIVES

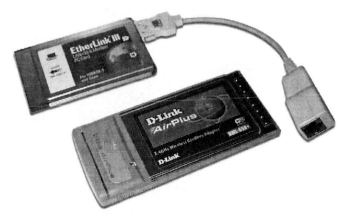

- A USB flash drive is a small box (about the size of a lighter) of flash memory which plugs into a USB port. Flash memory is a type of memory that can maintain its data without any external source of power, so it is an excellent way of storing documents, images and other files, and for transferring information from one computer to another. Digital cameras use this kind of flash memory in the form of cards of varying sizes.

- Once it is plugged in, the computer sees the USB drive as an additional hard drive. It is a highly-portable removable storage device that is sturdier than a floppy or CD-ROM.

- The storage capacity of a USB drive varies from 32 MB (for £20 or € 30) to 1 GB and up (starting at £150 or € 250).

## PCMCIA CARDS OR PC-CARDS

The photo above shows a network/modem card (at the top) and a wireless network card (below).

# Other external devices

▨ These are electronic cards that resemble credit cards. You can buy PCMCIA cards that perform diverse jobs such as:

- Network cards
- Modem cards
- Memory cards
- GPS navigation cards
- Interface cards with an external drive
- And so on.

▨ Network and modem cards are more and more built in to portable computers. External devices now frequently use USB ports. For these reasons, PCMCIA cards are now less popular.

Getting to know the hardaware

# 2<sup>nd</sup> Part

*Now that you know what makes up your computer, you are ready to discover the operating system. This is the working environment in which you will carry out all the tasks on your computer.*

## Discovering the environment

2.1 **The desktop** p.44

2.2 **Basic operations** p.52

# The desktop

*Windows is the name of the operating system on your computer. Your computer could not run without this basic software, as it would not be able to start. PCs (Personal Computers) run the Windows system, while Macintosh computers run a different operating system (Mac OS).*
*Windows XP is a multi-user system. This means that you can create several user accounts on it. In this way, several users can work on the same computer and each user can customise his/her workspace, without affecting the workspaces of the other users. Each user has an individual* **My Documents** *folder in which to keep the documents that he/she creates. The user can decide to allow, or not allow other users to access this folder.*

## STARTING WINDOWS XP

▓ When you start your computer, by default, the users of your computer appear in the Windows XP Welcome screen.

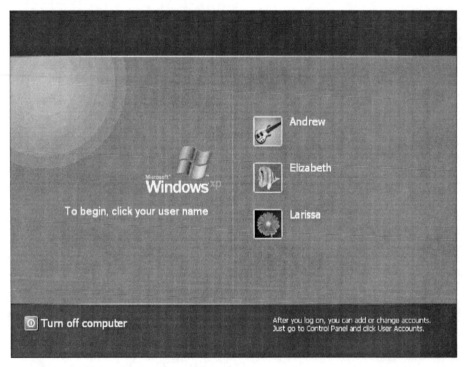

In the above example, three users have been created.

If you are the only user of the computer (if you have just bought your computer or if you have not yet created other user profiles, for example) then this screen will not appear: Windows XP will open your working session automatically and you will go straight into the Windows desktop. In this case, you can skip the rest of this section and go straight on to the next section, **Discovering the XP desktop**.

If several users have been created and you do not see the Windows XP Welcome screen, it means that this screen has been deactivated. In this case, to log on to the computer, you must enter your user name, and any password you may have, in the **Log On to Windows** dialog box.

▒ Otherwise, to log on, click your user name on the Welcome screen, as it prompts you to, then enter any password you may have. If you have forgotten your password, click the ![?] button to view any text you entered as a hint when you defined your password: this text should help you to remember your password.

When you enter your password, it appears as a set of dots.

▒ When you have finished entering your password, click the ![→] button or press the Enter key to validate it.

Your workspace or desktop appears on the screen.

# The desktop

*When you have logged on to your computer, the Windows desktop appears on the screen. This desktop provides access to the different items on your computer (it allows you to start Word or Works for example, or to access the files on your hard disk, etc.). The example below shows the desktop by default. However, as you can customize it, your desktop may appear differently.*

## DISCOVERING THE WINDOWS XP DESKTOP

* However, your desktop will always show the following items:

- the **taskbar** (a) provides a button to access each open application (in the above example, no applications have yet been opened). You can set the taskbar to hide itself when you are not using it or to show the Quick Launch bar, etc.

- the **start** button (b) provides access to the main Windows menu.

- the **notification area** (c) displays the system time along with a number of notification icons. For example, it may show an icon to let you know that you have received e-mail.

- the **Recycle Bin** (d) is there to receive the files you delete. By default, when you delete a file, the system transfers it to the **Recycle Bin**. This approach allows you to retrieve any files you deleted by mistake.

 The desktop may also show other icons (objects) such as shortcuts, which provide quick access to applications or files.

*You can generally access the different items on your computer in a number of different ways. For example, you may be able to start an application (such as Word or Excel) directly from your desktop, if it shows the corresponding icon. Otherwise, you can always start applications from the start menu.*

## START MENU

To display the Windows XP **start** menu, click the **start** button. Alternatively, you can press the ⊞ key or press Ctrl Esc on your keyboard.

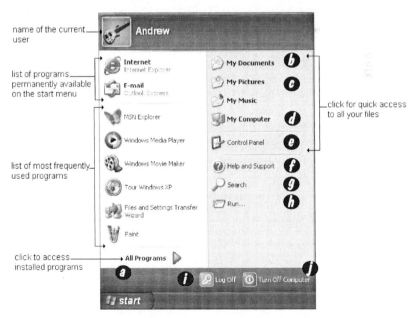

# The desktop

- By default, the main Windows XP **start** menu contains the following items:
  - The **All Programs** menu (a) lists all the applications installed on the computer.
  - The **My Documents** option (b) opens a window of the same name that contains two folders, by default: **My Music** and **My Pictures**. It is recommended that each user of the computer saves his/her documents in his/her **My Documents** folder.
  - The **My Music** and **My Pictures** options (c) provide direct access to the corresponding folders.
  - The **My Computer** option (d) provides access to all the components of your computer. These components are divided into different categories that depend on how your computer is set up.
  - The **Control Panel** option (e) opens a window of the same name that allows you to modify your working environment (by setting up your network connections, managing the user accounts, configuring your devices, adding or removing programs and so forth).
  - The **Help and Support** option (f) provides access to the Windows XP **Help and Support Center** application.
  - The **Search** option (g) provides access to a number of options that allow you to find files, folders, people (in an address book) and computers on the network. As its name suggests, you can use the **Search the Internet** option in the **Search Companion** bar to carry out a search on the Internet.
  - The **Run** option (h) allows you to run a program by specifying the corresponding executable file.
  - The **Log Off** option (i) closes the current session and allows another user to log on.
  - The **Turn Off Computer** option (j) opens the **Turn off computer** dialog box. This dialog box allows you to turn off your computer, to restart it or to put it into hibernation (Windows XP saves your desktop environment onto your hard disk before turning off your computer, so it can restore your desktop as you left it when you restart your computer).
- If you open the **start** menu by mistake, you can close it again by clicking anywhere on the desktop or by pressing Esc.

This chapter does not describe all the menus and options that the **start** menu provides. It concentrates on essential features. Feel free to explore the options and submenus yourself.

*Windows XP opens a session with customised settings for each user who logs on. When the user logs off, he/she closes his/her session along with all the files and applications opened. It is a good idea to close all open sessions before switching the computer off.*

## CLOSING A WINDOWS XP SESSION (LOGGING OFF)

▧ Click the **start** button followed by the **Log Off**  button.

▧ In the **Log Off Windows** dialog box that appears, click the **Log Off** button.

![Paint dialog box: "Save changes to logo?" with buttons Yes, No, Cancel]

If you leave a file open without saving modifications you have made to it, this type of message appears.

▧ If you see this type of message and you want to save your changes, click the **Yes** button. Otherwise, click the **No** button.

Windows saves your settings then displays the Welcome screen (or the **Log On to Windows** dialog box) to allow you to log on again. ENI Publishing provides a more advanced book in the Way In collection called Windows XP - Home Edition that describes how to create a new user account.

 If several people are logged on to your computer, they must all log off before you switch off the computer.

# The desktop

*To switch on your computer, you need only press its **Power** button. On the other hand, if you want to switch off your computer, you must first close any applications that are currently running.*

## SWITCHING OFF YOUR COMPUTER

▨ Close all current sessions (cf. Closing a Windows XP session (logging off)).

▨ Click the **start** button followed by the **Turn Off Computer** button.
The **Turn off computer** dialog box appears.

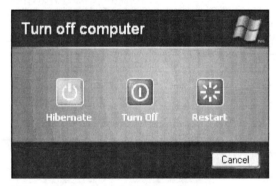

The **Cancel** button of this dialog box cancels this action.

The **Restart** button shuts down Windows and re-opens it immediately, while the

**Hibernate** button shuts down Windows after saving your desktop environment onto your hard disk (for example, it saves to your hard disk the layout of the windows on the screen and the state of any open applications so that it can open them in the same state the next time you restart your computer).

▨ Click the **Turn Off** button to close Windows so that you can switch off your computer.

▨ According to the type of computer, your computer will switch itself off automatically or Windows will advise you that it is safe to switch off your computer. In the latter case, press the **Power** button on the main unit of your computer (you may need to keep this button pressed in for several seconds before the computer switches off).

If any other users are still logged on when you attempt to shut down Windows, this message will appear:

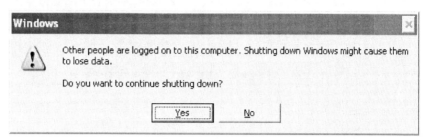

If you click **Yes**, the other users might lose data; if you click **No**, you will cancel your action.

# Basic operations

Once you have started your computer, you will not be content just to sit and admire your desktop! To start using your computer and set up your documents, you must open an application (or program). For example, if you want to write a letter, you may want to use a word processor such as Word, or if you want to make calculations, you may want to use a spreadsheet application such as Excel. To access an application you must be able to see it on the screen: you can then "start" or "run" the application.

## STARTING AN APPLICATION FROM THE START MENU

- Click the **start** button to open the main menu of Windows XP.
- If necessary, point to the **All Programs** option.
- If necessary, move the mouse pointer, to open the appropriate menu or submenu.
- Click the name of the application you want to run.

  The application window opens and the application's button appears on the taskbar:

For example, to start the **Notepad** application, click the **start** button, point to the **All Programs** option then to the **Accessories** menu and click the **Notepad** option.

Discovering the environment

The **Notepad** application is installed automatically when you install Windows: it allows you to write text with almost no formatting. If there is a **Notepad** icon on your desktop, you can also double-click this icon to start the application (for this reason these icons are called shortcuts).

 Programs that you have used recently may appear directly in the **start** menu. To run one of these programs, just open the **start** menu and click the name of the application.

*Every application appears in its own window. The window is the basic element of the Windows system (hence its name). All windows have a number of common items, with which you must be familiar.*

## GENERAL WINDOW ITEMS

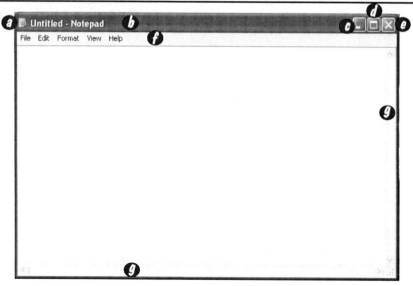

*The scroll bars (g) appear greyed-out because the window is empty.*

# Basic operations

▧ Every window has the following items:

- **Control menu** (a): open this menu to manage the window (by moving it or changing its size). In practice, this menu is hardly ever used, as you can carry out the actions it offers in more direct ways.

- The **title bar** (b) displays the name of the active document (in the above example, this "title" is **Untitled,** as this new document has not yet been saved to disk), followed by the name of the application (Notepad in this example).

- The **Minimize** (c) and **Maximize** (d) buttons collapse the window into its scroll bar button and enlarge the window to the full screen size, respectively.

- The **Close** button (e) closes the window and the application.

- The **Menu bar** (f) contains the different menus of the application; these menus are closed in this example.

- **Scroll bars** and **scroll cursors** (g) allow you to scroll through the contents of the window (the **scroll cursors** or **scroll boxes** do not appear in this example because the window is empty).

When you open a document, such as a letter you have already prepared, it appears in a document window within the application window.

*When you start a program, the application window may fill the screen (in this case it is said to be in "full-screen" mode). When an application window does not fill the screen, you can see the desktop in the background. If a window is in your way, you can resize it to make it smaller or move it to a more convenient position.*

## MOVING AND RESIZING A WINDOW

▧ To move a window, point to its title bar (b) then hold down the mouse button, drag to the required position and release the mouse button.

▧ To minimize the window (into its taskbar button) leaving the application active, click the ▬ button (c).

Here, the **Notepad** application window has been minimized.

▧ To restore one of your active windows, click its button on the taskbar.

- To enlarge the window so that it fills the screen, click the **Maximize** button on the window's title bar.

  **The window now covers the whole screen: only the taskbar remains visible (and you can hide this if you wish). The button is replaced by the Restore Down button.**

- To restore the window to its previous size, click the button.

- To change the height or width of a window that is not in full-screen mode, point to one of the edges of the window: to change the height <u>and</u> the width of the window, point to one of the corners of the window.

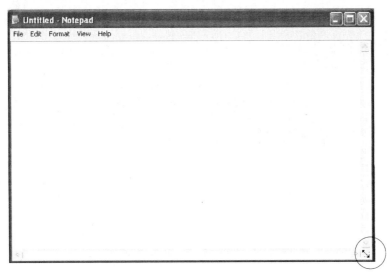

*The mouse pointer appears as a double-headed arrow.*

Hold down the mouse button and drag the mouse to resize the window as required, then release the mouse button.

*As you can run several applications at once, you can have several open windows that overlap each other. From time to time, you may need to "tidy your desktop".*

## MANAGING SEVERAL WINDOWS

- When several windows overlap, you can recognise the active window by the colour of its title bar. By default, the title bar of the active window is blue (while the title bars of inactive windows are light blue) and the taskbar button of the active application appears pressed-in.

# Basic operations

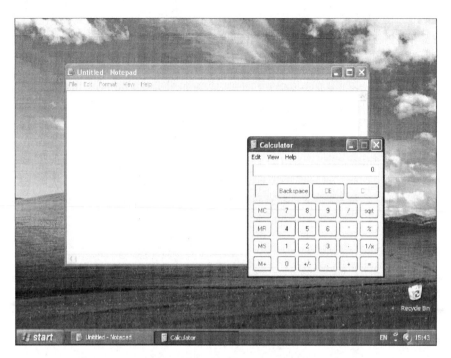

*For example, after you have started **Notepad**, run the **Calculator** application by clicking the **start** button, pointing to the **All Programs** option then to the **Accessories** menu and clicking **Calculator**.*

▨ To access a window and activate the corresponding application, click in the window if it is visible, or click its button on the taskbar, or hold down the ⌐Alt⌐ key and press the ⌐⇥⌐ key once or more until you select the icon corresponding to the window concerned.

The active window appears in the foreground.

To modify the window layout, right-click an empty space on the taskbar to view the menu that is associated with it:

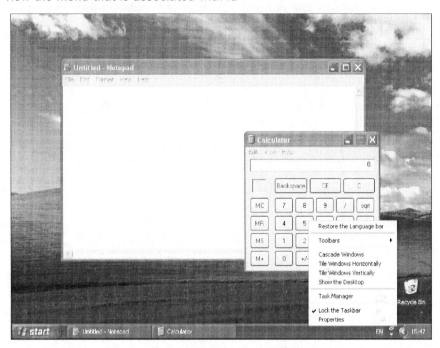

*The menu associated with the taskbar is called the taskbar's shortcut menu.*

Choose one of the following options:

**Cascade Windows** — to arrange the windows so that they overlap each other.

**Tile Windows Horizontally** — to arrange the windows so that they appear one underneath the other.

**Tile Windows Vertically** — to arrange the windows so that they appear side by side.

To minimize all the windows into their taskbar buttons, right-click an empty space on the taskbar and click the **Show the Desktop** option.

To restore all the windows you minimized when you chose the **Show the Desktop** option, display the taskbar shortcut menu and click the **Show Open Windows** option.

This action will restore your previous window layout.

# Basic operations

*You have started your application and perhaps maximized the application window to have as much space as possible: you are now ready to start working. According to the application you are using, you may start entering text or making calculations or doing a drawing. Whatever the application you are using, sooner or later you will need to use the menus that appear under the window's title bar. When you start the application, these menus are closed. To use one of these menus, start by opening it.*

## MANAGING AN APPLICATION'S MENUS AND OPTIONS

To open a menu, click its name on the menu bar.

The menu's options appear:

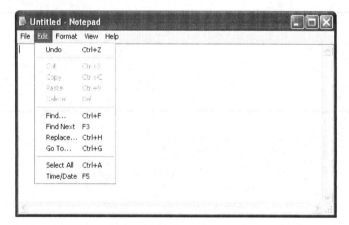

*For example, to open Notepad's **Edit** menu, click **Edit**.*

You cannot use the greyed-out options, as they are unavailable at the present time.

An ellipsis (...) to the right of an option indicates that you will see a dialog box when you choose the option.

- To open an adjacent menu, point to its name.

- To activate a menu option, slide the mouse up or down (without clicking) until you are pointing to the option, then click.

- To close a menu without activating one of its options, click elsewhere in the window.

To access the menu bar from the keyboard, press the Alt key or the F10 key.

This action selects the first menu on the menu bar, without opening it. One letter in each menu name appears underlined.

▓ To select an adjacent menu, press the ⊒ key or the ⊏ key. To open a menu that you have selected, press the [Enter] key or the ⬇ key.

▓ To open a menu directly, hold down the [Alt] key and press the underlined (mnemonic) letter for the menu concerned.

For example, in **Notepad**, the [Alt] **E** key combination opens the **Edit** menu.

▓ To activate a menu option, use the ⊒, ⊏, ⬆ and/or ⬇ keys to select the option then press the [Enter] key. Alternatively you can simply press the underlined letter for the option concerned (after having opened the menu concerned using one of the techniques described above).

For example, in **Notepad** use the [Alt] **E** key combination to open the **Edit** menu then press **D** to activate the **Time/Date** option.

Here are a few commonly-used terms and expressions: a **menu** is made up of **options**. To **run** (or **use** or **take**) **a command** means to open the appropriate menu and activate the option concerned: for example, to run the **File - Page Setup** command means to open the **File** menu and click the **Page Setup** option.

The shortcut key (key combination) shown to the right of some menu options allows you to run the option concerned without opening the menu. For example, in **Notepad**, the [F5] function key inserts the time and date into your document without you having to open the **Edit** menu and click the **Time/Date** option.

# Basic operations

*With some menu options a small new window may appear on your screen. With these menu options, an ellipsis (...) appears to the right of the option name indicating that the application needs further information before it can complete the action you require. For example, with the File - Page Setup command, you must indicate the paper format and orientation in which you want to print. These small windows are called dialog boxes. When a dialog box opens you must close it before you can return to your document and continue working on it.*

## FILLING IN DIALOG BOXES

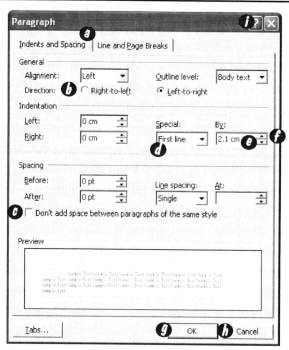

*This dialog box was chosen as an example because it offers more features than that which appears when you run the File - Page Setup command in the Notepad application.*

A dialog box can contain the following items:

- Tabs (a) provide access to the different pages in the dialog box.
- Option buttons (b) allow you to choose between different exclusive options; a black dot indicates the active option. Only one option can be active at the same time in the same group (such as the **Direction** group in the example).
- Check boxes (c): a tick in the check box indicates that the option is active; to activate or deactivate the option, click the check box.

- List boxes (d) allow you to choose from a list (the example shows a drop-down list box). Click the ▼ button to open the list box and choose a list item; click this button again to close the list box. An ordinary list box sometimes provides a scroll bar and arrows that you can use to scroll through the list contents (as in a window).
- Text boxes (e) allow you to enter information; if the text box accepts numbers it may contain increment buttons (f) that you can click to increase or decrease the displayed value.
- The **OK** button (g) closes the dialog box, keeping any changes you have made to the different options.
- The **Cancel** button (h) closes the dialog box, cancelling any changes you have made to the different options (clicking this button has the same effect as clicking the ✕ button).
- An **Apply** button sometimes appears in dialog boxes; it allows you to view the effects of your changes without closing the dialog box.
- The ? button allows you to view specific help information on the different items in the dialog box (see below).

▨ If your mouse breaks down, you can change the options in a dialog box using the keyboard. To access the different options you can use the ⇆ and Shift ⇆ keys; alternatively you can hold down the Alt key and press the letter that appears underlined for the option concerned.

▨ To move between the different options in a group or in a list, use the →, ←, ↑ and/or ↓ keys.
To activate or deactivate a check box, press the space bar.

*When you start an application, it appears in its own window. The easiest way to close an application is to close its window.*

## LEAVING AN APPLICATION (CLOSING A WINDOW)

▨ To close an application, click the ✕ button in the top right-hand corner of the application window or press the Alt F4 keys. Alternatively you can run the **File - Exit** command.

If the application window is minimized (if it appears only as a button on the taskbar) right-click its taskbar button and click the **Close** option.

# Basic operations

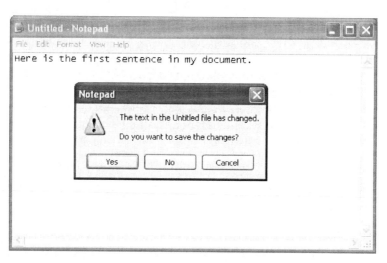

*If you try to close an application without saving all the changes you have made to your document, Windows asks you if you want to save your changes before closing the window.*

Click **Yes** to save your document, click **No** to close the application without saving your changes or click **Cancel** to cancel your action (in this case your document will stay open).

The next chapter explains how to save your documents.

 In general, documents open in document windows (within the application window). To close a document window, click the ☒ button in the top right-hand corner of the document window or press `Ctrl` `F4` (and not `Alt` `F4`) or run the **File - Close** command (and not the **File - Exit** command).

*Good knoledge of Windows is essential but you also need to work in different applications for different tasks, such as a spreadsheet, a word processor and so on. Here you will learn the basic functions of the Word word preocessing application and the spreadsheet included in the Works software suite.*

# 3rd Part

# Getting to know Word and Works

3.1 **Word: a word processor**     p.64

3.2 **Works: a software suite**     p.86

# Word: a word processor

*Word is a word processor. A word processor is an application that you can use to create, edit and print letters, reports and so forth. As the previous part described, you must first start (or run) an application before you can use it.*

## STARTING MICROSOFT WORD

▓ Click the **start** button on the taskbar at the bottom of the screen then point the mouse to the **All Programs** option.

The contents of the **All Programs** menu appear on the screen.

▓ Drag the pointer onto the **Microsoft Office** option to open the attached submenu.

▓ Click the **Microsoft Office Word 2003** option.

A introductory screen appears presenting the name of the application then the workscreen appears.

As with all applications, Word's features develop with each successive version: this chapter describes Word 2003 (the latest version that was available at the time of going to press). If you have an earlier version of Word (Word 97, 2000 or 2002) your screens will be slightly different from those presented here, but the basic operations that this chapter describes will generally be the same.

If there is a **Microsoft Word** shortcut icon on your desktop, you can also double-click this icon to start the application.

*The Word application appears in a window with whose layout you should already be familiar. However, this chapter will describe this window again to help you to get to know it better: remember that all applications use the same basic window layout.*

## GETTING STARTED WITH THE WORKSCREEN

The Word workscreen contains various items:

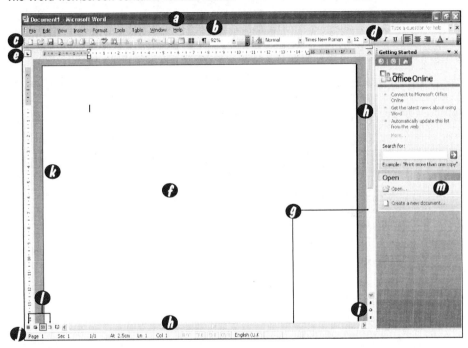

The title bar and its icons (a): on the left is Word's **Control** menu icon (W) followed by the name of the active document (here, **Document1** as it is a new document), followed by the name of the application (**Microsoft Word**). On the right, the **Minimize** button ( — ) reduces the window to its minimum size, into the taskbar, without closing the application; the **Restore Down** button reduces the window so that it does not necessarily occupy the whole screen. When you click the Restore Down button the **Maximize** button appears in its place; this button restores the window to full screen mode. Finally the **Close** button closes either the application or just the current document.

# Word: a word processor

**The menu bar (b)** contains the names of the various menus in the Word application and the **Type a question for help** box. You can type a question or a keyword in this box to see the corresponding help topics. The document's **Close window** button (☒) is to the right of this box.

**The Standard(c)** and **Formatting(d) toolbars** share the same line. You can use these toolbars to run quickly and easily some general Word commands, such as saving a document to disk. If these toolbars do not appear on your screen, you can activate the **Standard** and **Formatting** options in the **View - Toolbars** menu.

**The ruler (e)** lets you change the presentation of your text quickly. Show the ruler using **View - Ruler**.

**The work area (f)** is the space in which you enter and format your text.

**The scroll bars and cursors (g)/(h)**: the cursors in the scroll bars indicate the position of the insertion point in the document and allow you to view text that is longer or wider than the screen.

**The Select Browse Object button (i)** allows you to move around the document according to the items it contains. You can move, for example, from field to field or from end note to end note.

**The status bar (j)** contains information about the Word environment or the selected command.

**The selection bar (k)** is an invisible column that runs down the left of the document.

**The View buttons (l)** show the current document view and allow you to switch to a different view (Normal, Web Layout, Print Layout, Reading Layout or Outline).

**The task pane (m)** contains options for carrying out different tasks such as creating a new document, finding text, inserting clipart or creating a mail merge. By default, the **Getting Started** pane is open when you start Word. You can display the task pane using **View - Task Pane**.

*It is time to start your first text: this is called "entering" your text. Be careful: a word processor does not work in quite the same way as a typewriter! Although entering text may be fairly simple, you must still follow certain rules.*

## ENTERING TEXT

▨ To enter text in a document, click where you want to start.

▨ Type in your text. Word takes care of the line breaks: when the insertion point reaches the end of the line Word brings it back to the beginning of the next line automatically.

▨ To enter text in capitals, press the `Caps Lock` key to set the **Caps Lock** then enter your text as you would normally. To cancel the **Caps Lock**, either press the `Caps Lock` key again or press the `Shift` key, then carry on entering your text.

▨ To enter a single capital letter, at the beginning of a sentence for example, hold down the `Shift` key while you enter the letter concerned.

▨ To enter numerical values using the number pad, check that the **Num Lock** indicator is lit (if it is not lit, press the `Num Lock` key) then enter the numbers.

▨ When you enter the first characters of today's date, a day of the week, a month or certain set expressions that Word recognises, Word displays a ScreenTip showing the full expression (this is Word's autocomplete feature): either press the `Enter` key to accept Word's suggestion or just carry on typing.

▨ To start a new paragraph, press the `Enter` key.

The insertion point goes to the beginning of the next line. Your new paragraph will be aligned in the same way as the previous one.

▨ To leave space between two paragraphs, press the `Enter` key once or more.

Each time you press the `Enter` key, you create a new empty paragraph.

▨ Enter the text of your new paragraph.

▨ Carry on in this way until you have entered all your paragraphs of text.

# Word: a word processor

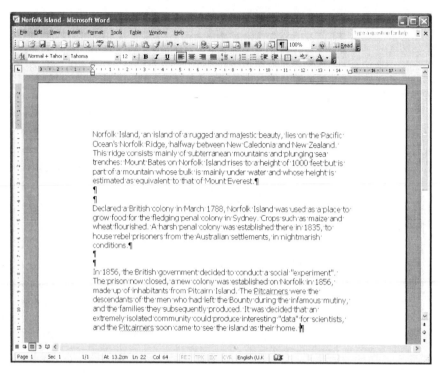

This text is made up of three paragraphs separated from each other by two empty paragraphs. This screen shows the end of paragraph symbol ¶ that marks each place you press the Enter key. The empty spaces at the top, on the left and on the right of the text are the margins that Word will apply when you print the document.

You can format your text either while you are entering it or after you have entered it. For example, you could change the alignment of a paragraph before you enter the text it must contain.

If Word underlines any of the words in your text in red, examine them carefully: they may contain spelling mistakes.

*The great advantage of a word processor over a typewriter is that with a word processor you can change any text you have entered, at any time. For example, if you forget a word in a sentence, there is no cause for alarm! You need only add the missing word in the appropriate place, provided that Insert mode is active!*

## USING INSERT/OVERTYPE MODE

When **Insert** mode is active, Word inserts any characters you enter between the existing characters. When you are in **Overtype** mode, new characters replace (or overtype) the existing ones.

▨ Before you enter the word you want to insert, check that the **OVR** indicator on the status bar appears in grey. If it appears in black, double-click this **OVR** indicator or press the ⌨Ins key.

▨ Enter the word(s) you want to insert.

▨ To deactivate insert mode and activate overwrite mode press the ⌨Ins key or double-click the **OVR** indicator again.

The letters **OVR** on the status bar change from grey to black. They indicate that you are now in overtype mode: the characters you enter replace existing characters.

▨ To return to insert mode press the ⌨Ins key or double-click the **OVR** indicator again.

*To shift to the right the next word you want to enter, resist the temptation of adding a number of spaces. If you subsequently change part of your document before this point, your text may no longer be correctly aligned. It is much better to insert a tab.*

## INSERTING A TAB

▨ Enter any text that must appear at the beginning of the line.

▨ To go to the next tab stop press the ⌨ key.

The insertion point moves to the right.

▨ To return to the previous tab stop, delete the preceding tab character by pressing the ⌨ key.

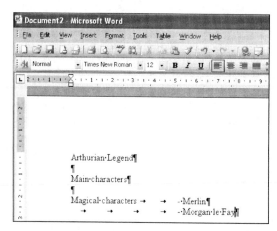

*This example shows two tabs before the name of each character. This technique ensures that the names will be perfectly aligned (this would not be the case had spaces been used instead).*

If you look at the example below, you can see that we tried to continue our list and something curious has happened. Word has suggested an automatic correction (automatic bullets), and displays an [icon] icon in the middle of the text. If you click this icon, there is a menu with which you can manage this AutoCorrect feature (rejecting the suggested change if you wish).

If you feel that Word's changes have improved the document, just keep typing to tacitly accept them.

 By default, Word sets tab stops every **1.27 cm** (or 1/2 inch). They are visible under the ruler as little grey vertical lines. When you show the nonprinting characters, Word represents the tab with the → symbol.

*As indicated above, the main advantage of the word processor is that you can use it to change text without crossing things out. For this, you need to know how to delete text.*

## DELETING TEXT

- Click to place the insertion point where you want to delete the text or select the text you want to delete (see "Moving the insertion point" and "Selecting text").

- To delete the character immediately before the insertion point, press the `←` key.

- To delete the character immediately after the insertion point, press the `Del` key.

- To delete a selected piece of text, press the `Del` key.

- To split a paragraph in two, place the insertion point just before what must become the first character of the new paragraph and press the `Enter` key.

- To merge two adjacent paragraphs, place the insertion point at the end of the first paragraph then press the `Del` key so as to delete the end of paragraph mark that separates the two paragraphs.

*As your text grows, you will need to move around in it, to edit it. For this purpose, you can use the navigation keys or the scroll bars on the scroll of the Word window.*

## MOVING THE INSERTION POINT

The insertion point is represented as a flashing vertical line. It marks your position in the document.

- Use the following keys to move the insertion point around:

| | |
|---|---|
| Next/previous character | `→`/`←` |
| Beginning of the next/previous word | `Ctrl` `→`/`Ctrl` `←` |
| End/beginning of the line | `End`/`Home` |
| Beginning of the next/previous paragraph | `Ctrl` `↓`/`Ctrl` `↑` |
| Bottom/top of the window | `Ctrl` `Alt` `PgDn`/`Ctrl` `Alt` `PgUp` |
| Next/previous window | `PgDn`/`PgUp` |
| Beginning/end of the document | `Ctrl` `Home`/`Ctrl` `End` |

# Word: a word processor

Use the scroll bars to reach the text which interests you:

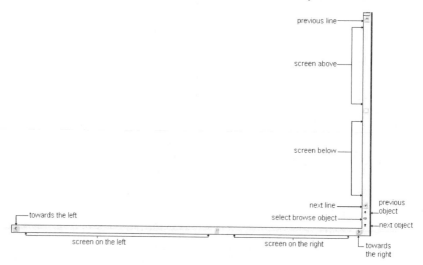

*If your document contains several pages, when you drag the scroll cursor, Word displays the number of the current page in the ScreenTip.*

To go straight to a specific point in the document, drag the scroll cursor along the scroll bar to that point's approximate position.

Now click in the text to place the insertion point.

You cannot go beyond the last characters entered at the end of the document.

*To apply the same operation to several words, lines or paragraphs, you do not need to work on each item separately. For example, if you want to move 10 paragraphs you do not need to move the paragraphs one at a time. It is quicker to select the 10 paragraphs concerned then move them all at once.*

## SELECTING TEXT

To select:

a word                                    double-click the word.

| | |
|---|---|
| a line | point at the left end of the line (the mouse pointer takes the form of an arrow pointing top right) and click once. |
| a paragraph | point at the left of the paragraph (the mouse pointer takes the form of an arrow pointing top right) and double-click. |
| a sentence | point at the sentence, hold down the Ctrl key and click once. |
| the whole document | point at the left edge of the text, and triple-click or hold down the Ctrl key and click once. |

▨ To select a group of characters:

| | |
|---|---|
| drag | click in front of the first character to be selected and, without releasing the mouse button, move over all the characters required. When the selection is correct, release the mouse button. |
| Shift-click | click in front of the first character that you want to select, hold down the Shift key and click after the last character required. |

**If you are using Word 2002 or later, you can select several distinct groups of text, by selecting the first piece of text, holding down Ctrl and selecting the other pieces of text (see example below).**

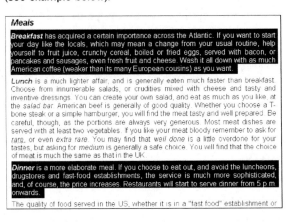

*Word highlights selected sections. When you make a fresh selection, Word cancels the previous selection.*

▨ Place the insertion point before the first character you want to select.

Hold down the Shift key as you use the direction keys to select (you can also press Ctrl Shift → to extend your current selection to include the next word).

# Word: a word processor

- When you are happy with the selection, release the `Shift` key.
- To select the whole document, use `Ctrl` **A** or the **Edit - Select All** command.

*Moving or copying any selection of text is a very useful feature of Word.*

## MOVING/COPYING TEXT

- Select the block of text you want to move or copy.
- To move the text, press `F2`; to copy the text, press `Shift` `F2`.

  On the status bar, Word asks **"Move to where"** for a move or **"Copy to where"** for a copy.

- Place the insertion point where you want to move or copy.
- Press the `Enter` key.

- Select the block of text you want to move or copy.
- Point to the selected text.
- If you want to copy the text, hold down the `Ctrl` key and drag so as to position the vertical grey line where you want to copy the text.
- If you want to move the text, simply drag to the position where you want to move the text.

  As you move text, a rectangle accompanies the mouse pointer; as you copy text a second rectangle containing a plus sign accompanies the mouse pointer.

*For the moment, your document is in the computer's central memory and nowhere else (in the RAM, which the first chapter described). If power suddenly cuts from your computer your document will disappear. To save your document you must store it on the hard disk of your computer.*

## SAVING A NEW DOCUMENT

- **File - Save** or 🖫 or `Ctrl` **S**

  The **Save As** dialog box appears. By default, Windows saves documents in the folder called **My Documents**.

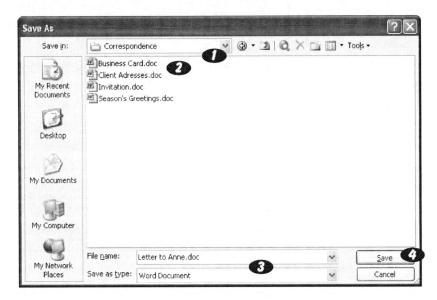

**1.** If you do not want to save your file in the folder that the **Save in** box suggests, click the arrow to open this list then choose the drive you want to use (for example, the C: icon generally represents your hard disk) and/or choose the folder that must accommodate your file (such as **Anne's Documents**, or **Shared Documents**, which all users can access).

**2.** If necessary, double-click the name of the folder in which you want to save your file: the name of this file appears in the **Save in** box.

**3.** In the **File name** box, enter the name you want to give to your document: a document name can be up to 255 characters long and can contain spaces (but it cannot contain \ / : < > or | characters).

**4.** Click to save your document.

The name of the document appears in the title bar. The file name extension may also appear: a Word document always has a .doc name extension, even if it is not always visible on the screen.

# Word: a word processor

You can use the **File - Save As** command to save your current document under a different name.

*When you want to continue working on a file you started yesterday for example, you must open your file from your hard disk.*

## OPENING A DOCUMENT

▨ **File - Open** or [icon] or [Ctrl] **O**

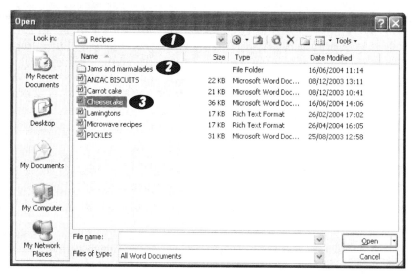

*1.* If the folder that the **Look in** box suggests does not contain the file you want to open, click the arrow to open this list then choose the drive concerned (for example, the **C:** icon generally represents your hard disk) and/or choose the folder that contains your file (such as the folder of another user or **Shared Documents**, which all users can access).

**2.** If necessary, double-click the name of the folder that contains your file. To access the parent folder (the next folder up in the hierarchy), click the  tool button.

**3.** Double-click the name of the document you want to open or select it then click the **Open** button.

To open one of the last documents you worked on, open the **File** menu and click the document's name at the end of the menu or click the link to the document in the **Open** area in the **Getting Started** task pane.

*As you work on your file, you will change it or add new information to it. You make these changes in the central memory (in the electronic circuits of your computer). You update the computer file on your hard disk each time you save your file. When you open your file, it is always in the state it was in when it was last saved. This means that if a power cut occurs, you will lose any changes you made since you last saved your file.*

## SAVING AN EXISTING DOCUMENT

▒ **File - Save** or 🖫 or Ctrl **S**

Windows does not display the **Save As** dialog box as your file already has a name and a storage location. Windows saves only the changes you have made.

*When you have finished working on a file, you can close it so as not to clutter up your computer's memory.*

## CLOSING A DOCUMENT

▒ Activate the document you want to close.

▒ **File - Close** or ✖ or Ctrl **W** or Alt F4

# Word: a word processor

If you try to close a document that you have not yet saved or that you have changed since you last saved it, the following message appears:

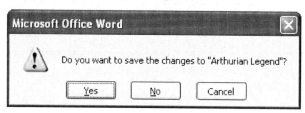

- Click the **Yes** button to save your file before you close it or click **No** to close your file without saving it or click **Cancel** not to close your document.

*When you have finished structuring your text, you may want to change its look to make it more pleasant to read or to highlight important words or phrases.*

## FORMATTING CHARACTERS

- If you have already entered the characters concerned, select them.
- Click one or more of the buttons on the **Formatting** bar to apply the attribute you require: **B** **Bold** type, *I* *Italics*, <u>U</u> <u>Underlined.</u>

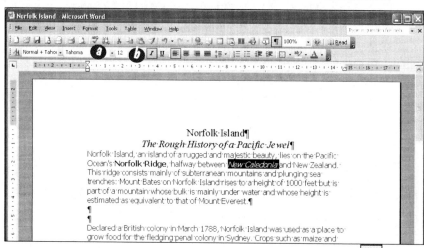

*In this example, italic style has been applied to "New Caledonia". The* I *button shows a blue border. You can apply several different formatting styles to the same text.*

- To deactivate a formatting style, click the corresponding tool button again.
- To change the font or the font style, open the corresponding list on the **Formatting** toolbar (a or b) then click the font or the font size you need.

You can format your characters while you type: activate the formatting style you require, enter your text in this format then deactivate the formatting style and continue typing your text.

- If you have already entered the characters concerned, select them.
- Use the following key combinations to apply the attributes you require:

| | | |
|---|---|---|
| Ctrl **B** | | **Bold** |
| Ctrl **I** | | *Italic* |
| Ctrl **U** | | Underlined |
| Ctrl Shift **D** | | Double Underlined |
| Ctrl Shift **W** | | Words only Underlined |
| Ctrl Shift **K** | | SMALL CAPITALS |
| Ctrl Shift **A** | | CAPITALS |
| Ctrl Shift **+** | | in $^{Superscript}$ (use the key on the alphanumerical keyboard) |
| Ctrl **=** | | in $_{Subscript}$ |
| Ctrl Shift **H** | | Hidden text |

- If the characters have already been entered, select them.
- **Format - Font** or Ctrl **D**

  The **Font** dialog box provides the full set of character formatting features.

- If necessary, activate the **Font** tab.

# Word: a word processor

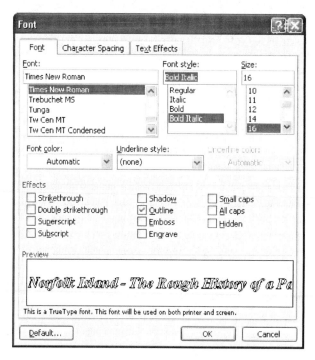

*In the **Preview** box, Word shows the text selected in the format chosen.*

Choose the formatting styles you require from the **Font**, **Font style**, **Size** and **Underline style** lists and from the **Effects** frame.

The illustration below shows the result of each effect:

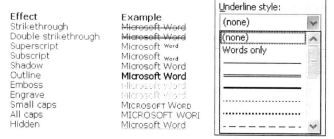

The **Underline Style** list offers several possibilities.

Click **OK** to confirm.

Getting to know Word and Works

*Now you have formatted your text, you may want to change its presentation by reformatting its paragraphs. This section explains how to align text with the left margin (Word aligns your text in this way by default) with the right margin or between these two margins (this type of alignment is often used for headings). You can even align your text with both of these margins at once (newspapers use this type of alignment and so does this paragraph you are reading).*

## CHANGING TEXT ALIGNMENT IN PARAGRAPHS

◾ Select the paragraphs whose alignment you want to change or if you want to re-align a single paragraph, simply click in it.

◾ According to the alignment you want to apply, click the corresponding button on the **Formatting** toolbar:

 left alignment (by default).

 centre alignment.

 right alignment.

 justified alignment: Word spaces the words out automatically to align the text with the left margin and with the right margin.

◾ Select the paragraphs whose alignment you want to change or if you want to re-align a single paragraph, simply click in it.

◾ **Format - Paragraph**

◾ Open the **Alignment** list then click the option corresponding to the required alignment.

◾ Click the **OK** button.

◾ Select the paragraphs whose alignment you want to change or if you want to re-align a single paragraph, simply click in it.

◾ According to the alignment you want to apply, use one of the following shortcut keys:

| | |
|---|---|
| Ctrl **L** | left alignment |
| Ctrl **E** | centre alignment |
| Ctrl **R** | right alignment |
| Ctrl **J** | justified alignment |

# Word: a word processor

You can also align the text in your paragraphs while you are entering your text. When you finish your current paragraph, press `Enter`. If the new paragraph requires the same alignment as the previous one, simply keep typing; if you wish to use a different type of alignment, choose the new type then enter the text for that paragraph.

*When you have finished your document, you may want to print it so that you can give it to other people. However, if you preview your whole document before you print it you will get a better result and save ink and paper: the print preview shows your document as Windows will print it.*

## STARTING THE PRINT PREVIEW

▓ **File - Print Preview** or [icon] or `Ctrl` `F2`

A reduced image of your document appears, as Word would print it. On the status bar, Word indicates the number of the page it is displaying.

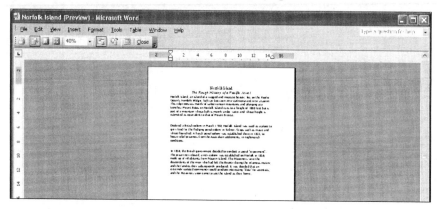

The **Print Preview** toolbar shows the current print preview zoom level.

▓ To view other pages of your document, use the vertical scroll bar or move from page to page using the `PgUp` and `PgDn` buttons.

▓ To return to the work area, click the **Close** button or press the `Esc` key.

You can start printing from the preview by clicking the  tool button.

*If you have already checked your document in the print preview or if you have printed your document before, you can start printing without concerning yourself with the page setup or with the print options.*

## PRINTING A DOCUMENT

▨ Click the 🖨 tool button.

The printing starts immediately according to the default settings that the **Print** dialog box defines.

*According to the length of your document, you may need several sheets of paper to print it. You can choose to print only that part of the document you have previously selected or only certain pages of your document (for example, suppose that your document will print on 4 pages and that you have just modified only the second page: rather than printing all four pages you can choose to print only the second page).*

## PRINTING PART OF A DOCUMENT

▨ To print a group of paragraphs, select them.

▨ **File - Print** or Ctrl **P**

# Word: a word processor

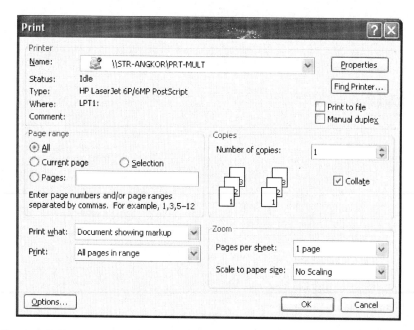

- To print the part of your text that you selected previously, click the **Selection** option in the **Page range** frame.

- To print only certain pages, access the **Pages** box in the **Page range** frame and enter the number(s) of the page(s) you want to print.

  To print a series of consecutive pages, enter the number of the first page then a dash then the number of the last page (for example, to print from page 5 to page 10, enter 5-10).

  If the pages you want to print are not consecutive, use commas to separate the page numbers (for example, to print page 5 and page 10, enter 5,10).

- To print the page in which the insertion point is currently positioned, activate the **Current page** option.

- To print only even or odd pages, select the corresponding option in the **Print** list.

- Click **OK** to confirm.

This section covers only Word's basic features. Of course, this highly sophisticated word processor offers many other features (column layouts, tables of contents, indexes, mail merges end so forth). Editions ENI offers books on Microsoft Word in other collections.

# Works: a software suite

Works often comes with the computer as standard supply. This application groups the Word processor that you have just looked at (to create and change text documents) a spreadsheet (to create and change tables) and a database management system (to create and use cross-referenced lists for storing data, such as information on catalogue items, for example). Works also includes other tools and applications for managing items such as your address book and your personal accounts. This chapter will describe the working environment that Works offers and the basic features of the spreadsheet application it provides.

## STARTING MICROSOFT WORKS

You can choose to run one of the applications integrated into Works (such as the spreadsheet, database or word processor), or you can go to a home page, called the Task Launcher, which offers several options (to create a letter or a budget, to open an existing document, etc).

### Starting a Works application

▨ To run one of the Works applications, click the **start** button, choose the **All Programs** option and point to the **Microsoft Works** option that is preceded by the ▧ symbol.

The contents of the Microsoft Works menu appear on the screen:

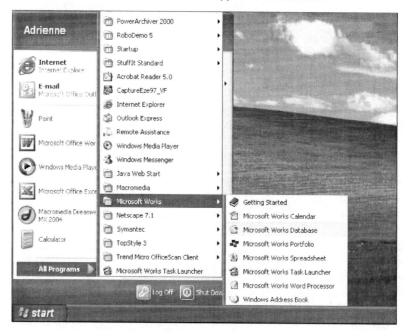

▧ Click the option that corresponds to the program you want to start: **Microsoft Works Calendar**, **Microsoft Works Database**, **Microsoft Works Spreadsheet**, **Microsoft Works Word Processor** or **Windows Address Book**.

## Accessing the Task Launcher

▧ Click the **start** button, choose the **All Programs** option and click the **Microsoft Works Task Launcher**, option with a  icon.

The **Home** page appears:

▧ To go to the **Task Launcher**, click the **Tasks** link on the navigation bar in the top part of the screen (a).

If you have a shortcut icon on your Windows Desktop, double-click it to start the **Task Launcher**.

# Works: a software suite

You have started the Task Launcher (see *Accessing the Task Launcher*) and you can now see its interface, which is a bit like a web page (as you will see in the chapter on the Internet). When you move the mouse around and point to a category, the mouse pointer becomes a hand with a pointing finger. This means that you are pointing at a hyperlink to a task, program or document (hyperlink is also an Internet term). If you click the link, you will open the task, program or document. In fact, the Task Launcher is the general menu for Microsoft Works. Below you can see how to use it.

## USING THE TASK LAUNCHER

### Launching a task

▨ To start a task, which means create a document using a template with the help of a "wizard":

**1.** Click the **Tasks** link (if you are not already in the Task Launcher).

**2.** Click the category that best describes the kind of task you want to find.

**3.** Click the task you want to start.

In the right of the window, the **Start this task** option appears.

▨ Click **Start this task**.

The wizard window appears. A wizard is a program that guides you through one or more steps to set up the task you have chosen.

Click the style of document you want, then click **Next** if the wizard is made up of several steps, or **Finish** if not.

If need be, follow the rest of the steps by selecting the options you want, then click **Finish**.

Microsoft Works starts the application that corresponds to the document you are creating.

## Starting an application directly

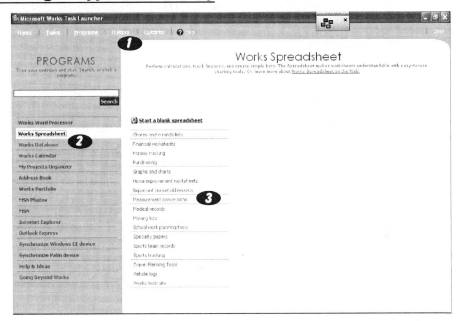

**1.** If necessary, click the **Programs** link in the **Microsoft Works Task Launcher** window.

**2.** Select the program you want. A list of tasks associated with this program appears to the right.

**3.** Click the **Start a blank "document type"** option if you want to open the corresponding application and create an empty document, or choose the task you want to perform, from the task list, and then click the **Start this task** option that appears.

If you use the first technique, a new document opens: if you choose a task, a wizard will help you to create a document using a template.

# Works: a software suite

*If you are working with a document and you want to enter new data elsewhere, you will have to create a new document.*

## CREATING A DOCUMENT

▨ In any of the Works programs, use **File - New** or press ⌨ Ctrl **N**.

The **Task Launcher** window appears.

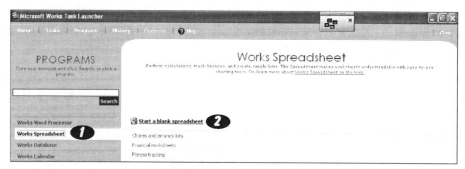

The program name selected in the left part of the screen corresponds to the program you were in when you used **File - New**.

*1.* If necessary, click the name of the program you want.

*2.* Click the **Start a blank "document type"** option.

A new, empty document appears on the screen.

 Click the ▯ tool button if you want to create a new document without returning to the Task Launcher.

To create your first table, you must start the Works Spreadsheet program and open a blank spreadsheet. You can do this via the Windows start menu or with the **Task Launcher**, as described on the previous pages. Like all Windows applications, the spreadsheet appears in a window. All windows have common features, with which you should be familiar.

## DESCRIPTION OF THE SPREADSHEET WINDOW

You can see only a small part of the Works spreadsheet, which contains **256** columns and **16384** rows (the last cell in the spreadsheet is called cell **IV16384**).

- The **title bar** (1) contains, on the left, the Spreadsheet's control menu icon (a), followed by its name and the name of the active spreadsheet. On the right are the **Minimize** (b), **Maximize** or **Restore** (c) and **Close** (d) buttons.

- The **menu bar** (2) contains all the Spreadsheet application's menus.
  Each menu provides options that you can use while you are working.

- The **toolbar** (3) supplies tools for carrying out actions or applying formats more rapidly. You can hide or display the toolbar using the **View - Toolbar - Show Toolbar** command.

# Works: a software suite

- The **entry bar** (4) shows the reference of the active cell; this is where you enter and edit data.

- The **work area** (5) is the space in which you work. It is made up of **cells**. The cells are created at the intersection of a column and a row, and their names are made up of the letter of the column and number of the row. When the pointer is in a cell, that cell becomes the **active cell** (6). It is surrounded by a black outline and its reference appears in the left of the entry bar. The black square you can see at the bottom right of the active cell is called the **fill handle** (7).

- The **scroll bars** (8) allow you to scroll the spreadsheet in the window.

- The **split box** (9) is used to split the window.

- The **status bar** (10) contains information about the keyboard or instructions about what you should do.

- By default, a Works **Help pane** (11) opens on the right edge of the window. You can use this to search for a help topic about the application. If you do not need this pane, you can close it with its ⊠ button (use F1 to open it at a later time).

*So here you are sitting in front of a spreadsheet. Before you can start entering data into the cells, you need to know how to go to the appropriate cell.*

## MOVING AROUND A SPREADSHEET

- Use the scroll bars to display the cell you want to activate then click in it, or use the following keys:

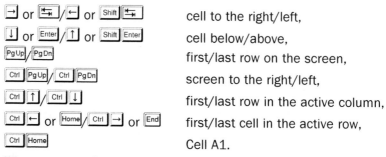

| | |
|---|---|
| → or ⇥/← or Shift ⇤ | cell to the right/left, |
| ↓ or Enter/↑ or Shift Enter | cell below/above, |
| PgUp/PgDn | first/last row on the screen, |
| Ctrl PgUp/ Ctrl PgDn | screen to the right/left, |
| Ctrl ↑/ Ctrl ↓ | first/last row in the active column, |
| Ctrl ← or Home/ Ctrl → or End | first/last cell in the active row, |
| Ctrl Home | Cell A1. |

When you move the mouse pointer around the spreadsheet, the name of the active cell appears at the beginning of the entry bar.

You can also use **Edit - Go To** or ⌘ **G** or 🔲, enter the reference of the cell you want, then click **Go to** or press 🔲.

*Now you are ready to create your first table. To create the table's cells, you will have to enter data into the spreadsheet's cells. These data can be of four different kinds: text, numbers, dates (Works knows there is no such date as 32/14/01!), and of course, calculations.*

## ENTERING DATA

▨ Activate the cell that will contain the data.

▨ Type the data. If you make a mistake, undo it by pressing 🔲.

As soon as you type the first character, three buttons appear on the entry bar:

 (equivalent to 🔲) confirms the data,

 (the same as 🔲) cancels the data,

 displays the help window.

▨ Confirm the data or activate the next cell.

As soon as they are confirmed, Text data are aligned at the left of the cell and Number and Date data are aligned on the right.

▨ Keep the following points in mind:

- to enter a negative value, precede it with a minus sign (-) or place it between brackets.
- to enter a number as a currency value, type the currency symbol then the number.
- enter a percentage by typing % just after the number.
- to enter decimal values, use the decimal separator specified in your Windows settings (usually the point).
- type times as follows: HH:MM:SS (e.g. 14:30:55).
- for dates, use any of the following formats: 02/02/95, 02/02, 02/95, 2 February 1995, February, 2 February, February 95. For year values entered as two figures, Works interprets them as follows: 00 to 29 correspond to 2000 to 2029, 30 to 99 correspond to 1930 to 1999.

*It is easy to make mistakes as you enter data, so it is a good idea to know how to change a cell's contents.*

## EDITING THE CONTENTS OF A CELL

▨ Activate the cell you want to edit.

**The cell contents appear in the entry bar.**

▨ Press [F2] or double-click in the cell, or click in the entry bar in the appropriate place.

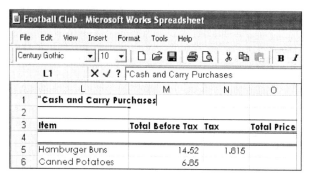

*Text data is preceded by an opening quotation mark (").*

▨ Make the necessary changes (such as adding or deleting characters) then confirm (click ✓ or press [Enter]).

You will often find that you need to change cell contents and sometimes you will want to delete them.

## DELETING THE CONTENTS OF A CELL

▓ Select the cell(s) concerned and press ⌷Del⌷. If you would rather use the mouse, you can also drag the fill handle back over the cells you have just selected.

*The Works Spreadsheet was created to calculate formulas. However, it is not a calculator. If you ask it to calculate (14879/45.5877 + 961413.458/56789.45), you will get an answer, but you would do better to go and find your calculator (or use the Windows **Calculator** application).*
*The formulas that you can enter are based not on the numbers contained in the cells but on the references of the cells themselves. This means that, if you make a change to the cell contents, the result of the formula will be updated automatically, without any intervention on your part.*

## ENTERING A CALCULATION FORMULA

▓ Activate the cell that is to contain the result and type a =.

▓ Move the pointer to the first cell you want to include in the calculation.

▓ Type the mathematical operator to be used:
+ (addition), - (subtraction), * (multiplication), / (division) or ^ (raising to power).

▓ In the same way, activate each cell that is to be included and add the appropriate mathematical operator.

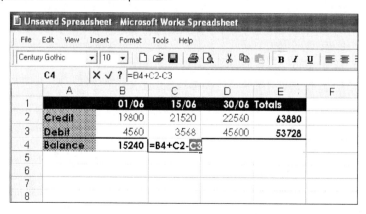

The calculation formula appears in the entry bar. The selected cell appears with a black background, and the status bar indicates that you are in **EDIT** mode.

▨ When you have inserted the last cell, use ☑ or Enter to confirm.

The result is visible in the cell, but the true content of the cell is the formula, which you can see in the entry bar when the cell is active. This is why, if you change any of the data in the cells in the formula, the result changes at the same time.

 You can also use the keyboard simply to type in the references of the cells that you want to include, instead of clicking them with the mouse or using the arrow keys.

Works offers an impressive range of formulas, or functions. You can apply these functions to a set of adjoining cells (called a cell range). For example you can calculate the sum of the values they contain, their average or their standard deviation. You can also apply trigonometric functions, to calculate the cosine of an angle, for example.

## INSERTING A FUNCTION INTO A FORMULA

▨ Activate the cell that is to contain the function.

▨ **Insert - Function**

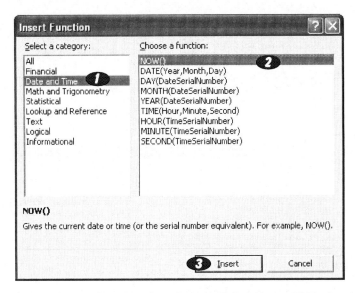

*The NOW() function inserts today's date in the selected cell (this date is then updated automatically).*

**1.** Under **Select a category**, choose the function you want (choose **All** to see a list of all the functions).

**2.** Click the name of the function you want to use and a description of the function appears in the bottom of the dialog box.

**3.** Insert the function into the active cell.

▒ Finish the formula and confirm.

*When you create tables, it is quite common that cells will have the same contents. Rather than taking the time to enter text or formulas over and over again, you can ask Works to reproduce your data in the appropriate cells. This is a technique known as "filling". Whether you are filling 10 or 500 cells, the data appears immediately.*

## COPYING THE CONTENTS OF A CELL TO ADJACENT CELLS

▒ To copy the contents of a cell to the cells below, select the cell whose contents you want to copy and also the destination cells, then use **Edit - Fill Down**.

▒ To copy the contents of a cell to the cells to the right, select the cell in question and also the destination cells and use **Edit - Fill Right**.

If you want to copy a cell's contents to any other cells, activate the cell in question then point to its fill handle so that a cross and the text FILL appear. Now drag the pointer as far as the last destination cell.

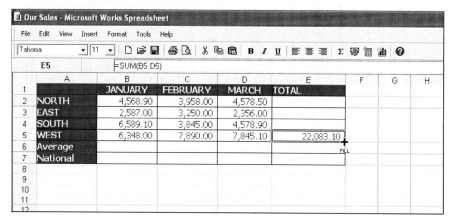

By dragging upwards, you will copy the calculation formula from cell E5 to the cells above.

*If you have almost finished your table, but now realise that you have forgotten a row, there is no need to fret. In Works, you can easily insert blank rows and columns between existing ones.*

## INSERTING ROWS/COLUMNS

- If you want to insert one row (or column), click in the row (or column) that will come after the new row (or column).
- If you want to insert several rows (or columns), select as many rows (or columns) as you want to insert.
- **Insert - Insert Row** or **Insert Column** or `Ctrl` `Shift` **+**

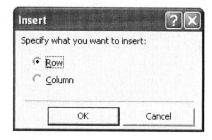

- Choose one of these options.

▓ Click the **OK** button.

Works inserts a new row (or column) and moves the selected cells downwards (or to the right).

*Not only can you insert rows and columns, you can also delete any rows or columns that you no longer need.*

## DELETING ROWS/COLUMNS

▓ Select a cell in each row or column you want to delete.

▓ **Insert - Delete Row** or **Delete Column** or ⌷Ctrl⌷ -

Be careful, because Works does not ask for confirmation and immediately deletes the rows or columns and their contents. If you make a mistake, use **Edit - Undo Delete Row** or **Undo Delete Column**.

*If you have typed a long text into a cell, only the first characters will be visible. The rest of the text is not lost however: by increasing the column width, you will be able to see the whole text.*

## CHANGING COLUMN WIDTHS

▓ To increase or decrease the width of a column manually, point to the vertical line you can see to the right of the column letter.

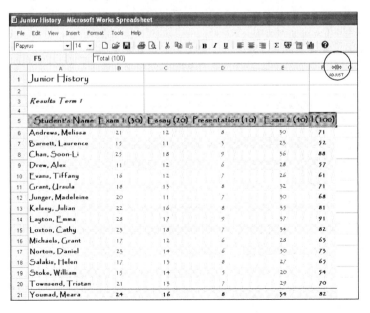

The mouse pointer takes this ⬱ shape: ADJUST.

- Drag to change the column width.

- To adjust the column width to fit its contents, double-click the column header.

- If you want a set of columns to have the same width, select them and use **Format - Column Width**. In the text box, type the number of characters you want as the column width, then click **OK** to confirm.

When a cell contains numerical data and the column is too narrow to display the entire cell contents, you will see that the numbers are replaced by hash symbols (#). If you increase the column width, the numbers will appear correctly.

*In the same way as you can change the width of columns, you can also change the height of rows.*

## CHANGING ROW HEIGHTS

- To change a row's height manually, point to the vertical line under the row's number, so that the mouse pointer takes this shape: ⭥ADJUST then drag.

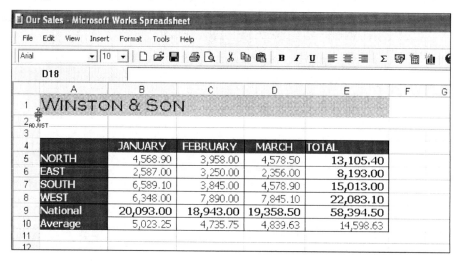

- To adjust the row's height to fit its contents, double-click the row number.

■ If you want several rows to have the same height, select them then use **Format - Row Height**.

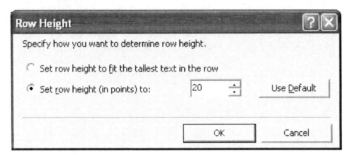

In the text box, enter the number of points you want for the row height.

The **Use Default** button will apply the default height to the selection and the **Set row height to fit the tallest text in the row** option will adjust the selected rows to fit their contents.

■ Click **OK**.

*After you have entered all the data into your table, you may want to format this data (for example, you may want to use larger characters for your totals).*

## FORMATTING CHARACTERS

■ Select the cells whose characters you want to format.

■ To change the font or the font size, click (a) or (b) to open the corresponding list then click the font or the font size you require.

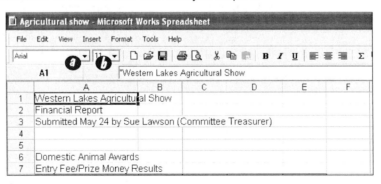

▓ You can choose from the following character styles:

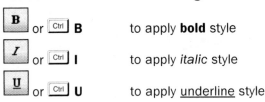

| | |
|---|---|
| **B** or Ctrl **B** | to apply **bold** style |
| *I* or Ctrl **I** | to apply *italic* style |
| U or Ctrl **U** | to apply <u>underline</u> style |

▓ Repeat the same action on the cell to cancel the style.

▓ Select the cells whose characters you want to format.

▓ **Format - Font**

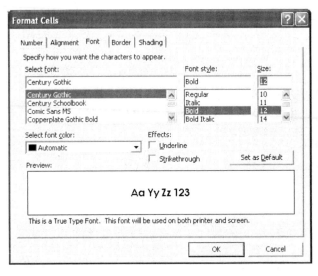

*You need to use this command only to apply **Strikethrough** style and to change the font colour. You can use the **Number** page of this dialog box to format numerical values and the **Border** page to apply a border around selected cells.*

▓ Activate the different formatting options you want to apply to the cells you selected.

▓ Click **OK** to confirm your settings.

When you start a new document in an application, Windows stores the data you enter in the computer's central memory: if your computer powers down you will lose all this data. So as not to lose this information you must store it on your computer's hard disk. You open, save and close a Works file as you would a Word file. The chapter on Word describes these operations in detail (cf. Saving a new document, Opening a document, Saving an existing document and Closing a document, on pages 74 to 78).

## SAVING, OPENING AND CLOSING A WORKS DOCUMENT

As with Word, use the following commands for these purposes:

▨ To save the document on which you are working:

**File - Save** or  or Ctrl **S**

▨ To save the document under a new name:

**File - Save As** or F12

▨ To open a document you saved previously:

**File - Open** or 🖃 or Ctrl **O**

▨ To close a document:

**File - Close** or ❎ or Ctrl F4

You will save paper and ink if you use the print preview, before you print your spreadsheet, this feature will show you a preview of the document exactly as it will print on paper.

## USING THE PRINT PREVIEW

▨ **File - Print Preview** or

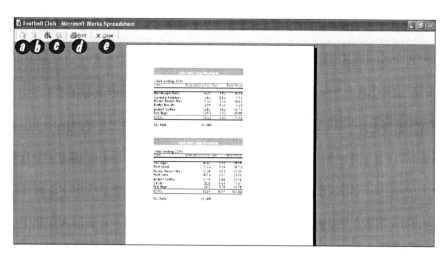

▓ Use the following buttons:

(a)  to see the next page,

(b)  to see the previous page,

(c)  to change the zoom,

(d)  to print the document,

(e)  to return to the document window.

*If you have already printed your document, or if you have already checked the print preview, you can go ahead and print without worrying about the page layout or the print options.*

## PRINTING A DOCUMENT

▓ **File - Print** or ⌐Ctrl⌐ **P**

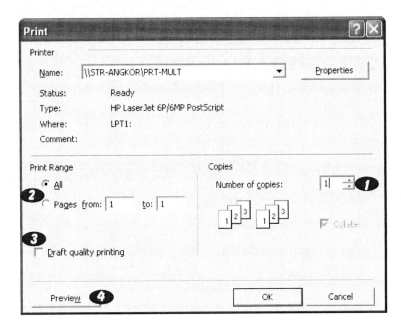

**1.** Indicate how many copies you want.

**2.** In the **Print Range** frame, click **Pages** if you only want to print a selection of pages and, in **from** and **to**, enter the numbers of the first and last pages you want to print.

**3.** In the spreadsheet and the database, you can activate the **Draft quality printing** option to speed up the printing (charts, database forms, drawings and so forth will not be printed).

**4.** Click **OK** to start printing, or choose **Preview** if you want to check the print preview.

 Use the ⌨ tool button to print without passing by the **Print** dialog box.

# Works: a software suite

*When you have finished using a Works application, you will want to close it. The way to do this is to close the application window.*

## CLOSING WORKS APPLICATIONS

▪ **File - Exit** or click the ☒ button on the application window, or press `Alt` `F4`.

If you try to leave an application before you save changes you have made to the open document, a message appears to remind you of this situation.

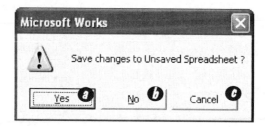

(a)    Saves the document.

(b)    Closes the application without saving the document.

(c)    Keeps the application open.

▪ If your document has never been saved, Works will suggest you save the document and give it a name.

When you work with your word processor or spreadsheet, you save your work as documents, or files. But how do you find your way around the files stored on the computer? How do you delete a file or copy it onto a disk? To carry out this type of task, you can use the Windows Explorer which you access with the My Documents window.

# 4th Part

## Windows XP

4.1 **My Documents window**          p.108

4.2 **Managing folders and files**   p.116

4.3 **Installing**                    p.130

4.4 **The Briefcase**                 p.138

# My Documents window

For each user of your computer, Windows XP creates an individual folder called **My Documents**, in which the user can store all his/her files (letters, workbooks, pictures and so forth). By default, the **My Documents** folder contains two subfolders: **My Pictures** and **My Music**. These subfolders contain sample pictures and music. Naturally, each user can create other subfolders in his/her **My Documents** folder (cf. Managing folders and files - Creating a folder).

If you wish, you can allow other computer users to access your personal (**My Documents**) folder and its subfolders or you can make these folders private by forbidding all other users from accessing your personal data. If several users can access your computer, Windows XP identifies the different personal folders according to the name of the user concerned. For example, suppose a computer has two users, Beatrice and Benedick: when Beatrice is logged on to the computer, her personal folder is called **My Documents**, while Benedick's personal folder appears under the name of **Benedick's Documents** (Beatrice can view Benedick's personal folder in the **My Computer** window by choosing **start** - **My Computer**). Windows identifies the **My Pictures** and **My Music** folders in the same way: when Beatrice is logged on to the computer, Benedick's **My Pictures** and **My Music** folders appear under the names of **Benedick's Pictures** and **Benedick's Music**, respectively.

## DISCOVERING THE MY DOCUMENTS WINDOW

▓ To open the **My Documents** window, click the **start** button on the taskbar then click the **My Documents** option.

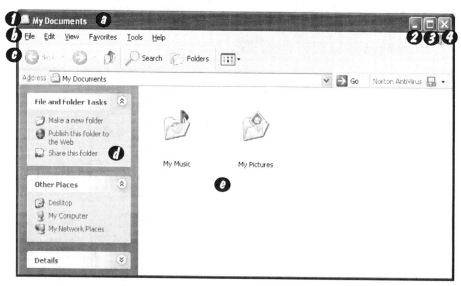

By default, the **My Documents** window contains only the **My Pictures** and **My Music** subfolders. You can create other folders in the **My Documents** folder and thereby add them to this list of existing subfolders.

The **My Documents** window contains the following items:

- the **title bar** (a) contains the **Control** menu (1), which allows you to manage the **My Documents** window, followed by the name of the selected folder (the **My Documents** folder in this case). On the right hand end of the title bar, the **Minimize** (2) and **Maximize** (3) buttons collapse the window into its scroll bar button and enlarge the window to the full screen size, respectively, while the **Close** button (4) closes the window.
- the **menu bar** (b) contains the different menus for managing the contents of the window.
- the **Standard Buttons** toolbar (c) contains tool buttons to carry out certain actions quickly.
- the left hand pane (d) contains several list boxes showing options that carry out certain actions when you click them. Five types of list boxes may appear: **File and Folder Tasks**, **Other Places**, **Picture Tasks**, **Music Tasks**, and **Details**. These boxes will offer different options according to the window item you select. If you cannot see the options that a box contains, click the ⌄ button on the right of the box's title bar. Similarly, to hide a box's options, click the ⌃ button, which appears in the same position.
- the right hand pane (e) shows all the folders and files in the folder concerned (this example shows the contents of the **My Documents** folder).

*When you open a folder window, by default, Windows displays a frame containing a set of boxes and each box offers a set of options that carry out various actions. You can replace this pane by one of five explorer bars. For example, the **Folders** explorer bar shows your computer's folder hierarchy (the full set of folders and files that your hard disk contains) and allows you to copy, move, delete, rename or search for folders and files.*

## DISPLAYING AN EXPLORER BAR IN A FOLDER WINDOW

Open the folder window in which you want to display an explorer bar (for example, the **My Documents** folder window, or the window of a subfolder of the **My Documents** folder).

Click the **View** menu and point to the **Explorer Bar** option.

Click the name of the explorer bar you want to display:

- the **Search** bar allows you to search for folders, files, people or computers in your computing network. It also allows you to search the Internet.

# My Documents window

- the **Favorites** bar lists all your favourite pages (whether they are on the Internet or not). You can add new page items to the list in this bar to make it easier to access these pages in the future. You can group your pages according to common themes by organizing them into different folders.
- the **Media** bar allows you to read music, video and multimedia files from the same folder window. It also provides access to the different media that the computer offers, such as Internet radio stations, for example.
- the **History** bar shows the pages (Web pages, Windows Help pages, documents and so forth) that you have visited today or in preceding days or weeks.
- the **Folders** bar displays the hierarchical structure of your computer's files, folders and devices and allows you to manage these items (by copying, moving, deleting, renaming and finding your files and folders, for example). You can also display this bar using the **start - All Programs - Accessories - Windows Explorer** command.

▧ To close an explorer bar, click the ✕ button in the top right corner of the bar.

*Although it is recommended that you work in the **My Documents** folder, you may still need to access folders other than those that your **My Documents** folder contains. For example, you may need to access another user's folders, or another drive such as a floppy-disk or a CD-ROM. For this purpose, you can use the **Folders** explorer bar, which displays the complete hierarchy of your hard disk.*

## ACCESSING A DRIVE OR A FOLDER

▧ Open the folder window of your choice.

▧ Display the **Folders** explorer bar either by using the **View - Explorer Bar - Folders** command or by clicking the [Folders] button on the **Standard Buttons** toolbar.

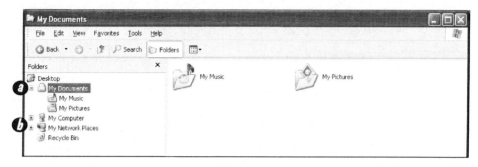

The right hand pane displays the contents of the item selected in the **Folders** bar. In this example, you see the contents of the **My Documents** folder, which is selected in the **Folders** bar.

In the example below, the **Folders** bar shows the different items of the desktop as a hierarchy: some branches of the hierarchy are expanded (a) to show the folder objects they contain, while other branches are collapsed (b). A minus sign (-) indicates an expanded branch, while a plus sign (+) indicates a collapsed branch. To expand or collapse a branch just click the + or the -. To expand a branch fully, click the folder concerned then press the * key (on the number pad).

In the **Folders** bar, click **My Computer** to display the items it contains.

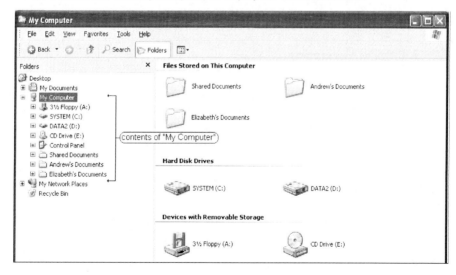

# My Documents window

The items contained in **My Computer** will vary according to the installation. However, they are generally grouped into the following categories:

- **Files Stored on This Computer** groups the folders that contain your working files.

- **Hard Disk Drives** groups your computer's hard disk drives (this example shows two hard disk drives: C: and D:).

- **Devices with Removable Storage** groups drives on your computer into which you can insert and withdraw storage units, such as floppy-disks and CD-ROMs.

Notice that different categories use different icon styles to portray their items.

To view the contents of a folder or a device, click the folder or the device in the explorer bar or double-click its icon in the right-hand pane.

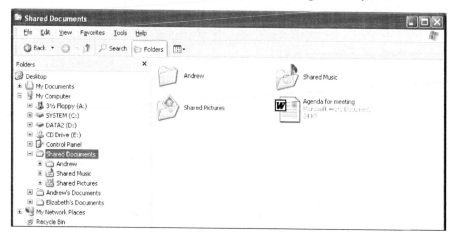

In this example, **Shared Documents** was clicked to show all the folders and files that this folder contains in the right hand pane.

To help you to distinguish a folder from a file, remember that a folder is used to store subfolders and files. A folder works in a similar way to a physical folder, which may contain dividers ("subfolders") with documents ("files") between them. A folder is always represented by this style of icon: 🗀. On the other hand, the icon for a file will vary according to the application that created it.

A folder that is not preceded by a + or - sign indicates that the folder does not contain any subfolders. However, the folder may still contain files.

When you open (expand) a folder, its icon changes (as with the **Shared Documents** folder in the example above).

▓ To access the folder on the next level up (the parent folder) you can run the

**View - Go To - Up One Level** command. Alternatively, you can click the button on the **Standard Buttons** toolbar or press the backspace ⌫ key.

In the example above, clicking the tool button will display the contents of **My Computer**.

▓ To go back to the folder or device you viewed previously, you can run the

**View - Go To - Back** command. Alternatively, you can click the ⊙ Back ▾ tool button on the **Standard Buttons** toolbar or press the Alt ⬅ shortcut key.

▓ To go forward again to the next folder or device in the list of those you viewed, you can run the **View - Go To - Forward** command. Alternatively, you

can click the ⊙ button or press the Alt ➡ shortcut key.

▓ To view again one of the folders or devices you viewed since you opened the

folder window, click the down-arrow on the ⊙ Back ▾ or ⊙ tool button then click the name of the folder or device you want to view again.

When a folder or drive appears in the right pane, you can double-click it to view its contents.

 To refresh the contents of the window so that it will take into account any changes that have occurred since you opened the window, use the **View - Refresh** command or press the F5 key.

*By default, a folder window shows the name of each file along with its size, its type and a file type icon. You can change this display, for example, to view only the icon or the name of each file or to view a thumbnail (miniature) of each file.*

## CHANGING THE PRESENTATION OF THE FOLDER/FILE LIST

▓ Select the folder whose presentation you want to change.

▓ Open the **View** menu or click the button.

# My Documents window

- You can choose from one of six options:

**Filmstrip**   available only for picture folders, this option presents each picture as a thumbnail, along with its name, in a single line. When you select a picture, a larger scale preview appears in a pane above.

**Thumbnails**   presents a preview picture and the name of each file in the folder. Pictures appear as thumbnails, while other types of file appear as the logo of the application that created them.

**Tiles**   shows the name of each file along with its type, size and a file type icon.

**Icons**   shows only the name of each file underneath an icon representing its type.

**List**   shows only the name of each file beside an icon representing its type. The files appear in the form of an ordered list in one or more columns (in alphabetical order by default). You cannot move the files to different positions in the list.

**Details**   lists the files in a single column showing an icon representing the type of each file along with other information including its name, its size, its type and the date and time it was last modified.

The example below shows the contents of the **Correspondence** folder in **Details** view.

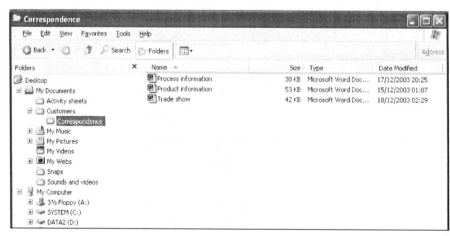

This view shows the size of each file in **kilobytes (KB)**: a byte is the space that one character occupies. The type of a file is associated with its format, which depends on the application that created the file. The icon preceding the file also depends on the application that created it, as does the filename extension (this is a set of three characters that appears as a suffix to the filename: by default, the filename extension does not appear in the folder window). The date and time of the last modification shows the system time when the file was last modified (your computer has an internal clock, which it uses for this sort of information).

▪ If any information in a column is not entirely visible, an ellipsis (...) appears at the end of the content (as in the **Type** column, in the above example). To view the content of a column in its entirety, you must widen the column concerned. You can do this by dragging the vertical separator line that appears to the right of the column header (for example, to the right of the **Type** header, above).

▪ To change the order in which the files appear in the list, use **View - Arrange Icons by** then click **Name**, **Size**, **Type** or **Modified** (date of last modification) according to how you want to sort the list.

▪ When your files appear in **Details** view, you can simply click the header of the column on which you want to sort. For example, clicking the **Date Modified** header will sort your files according to the date and time they were last modified. Click once to sort in ascending order; click again to sort in descending order.

# Managing files and folders

*Even if you have just bought your computer, your hard disk will not be empty: it will contain the files of the Windows XP operating system. These files are grouped together into folders. Your personal folder is present on the hard disk under the name of **My Documents**. This folder is there to accommodate the files you will create. When you have created a certain number of files, you may have trouble finding a specific document. To avoid long searches, it is recommended that you store your files in different folders that you can create for this purpose within your **My Documents** folder. Each of these folders can represent a certain theme or contain a certain type of file. For example, you could store all your files concerning your budget in a folder called **Budget**, or you could store all your letters in a folder called **Correspondence**. To draw an analogy, it is better to store your clothes on different shelves in a wardrobe than to keep them all together in a trunk.*

## CREATING A FOLDER

▒ To create a new folder in your **My Documents** folder, open the **My Documents** folder directly. For this purpose, click the **start** button followed by the **My Documents** option.

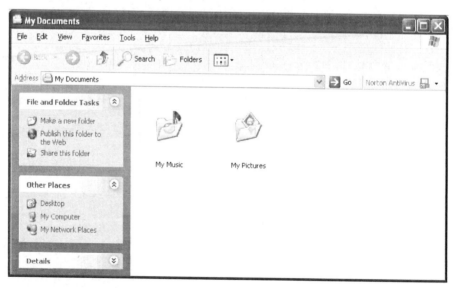

The **My Documents** window appears on the screen. Its left pane offers a number of options in the form of hyperlinks.

▒ To create a folder in your **My Documents** folder (on the same level as the **My Music** folder and the **My Pictures** folder) do not select any folder or file in the **My Documents** window.

To create a subfolder of an existing folder, double-click the folder concerned (for example, the **My Pictures** folder).

Windows XP

▓ Click the **Make a new folder** link in the **File and Folder Tasks** box in the left pane (if the options of this box are not visible, click the ⊗ button first). If your **File and Folder Tasks** box does not offer a **Make a new folder** link, you must have already selected a folder or file in the window. Deselect this folder or file by clicking an empty space in the right hand pane that is not occupied by any particular folder or file.

Alternatively, you can right-click an empty space of the right hand pane then choose the **New** option followed by the **Folder** option.

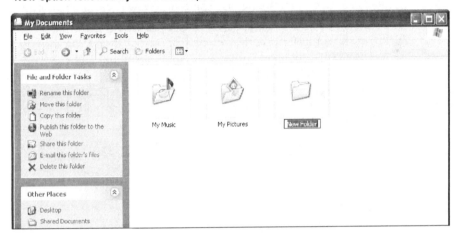

A new icon appears in the right pane. This folder is called **New Folder** for the moment: this name is highlighted and the insertion point blinks at the end of it, indicating that you can change it.

▓ Enter the name of your new folder: your name can be up to 255 characters long, including spaces. You can use uppercase or lowercase letters, or both, but you cannot insert the following characters: \ / ? : * " < > or |.

▓ Press the [Enter] key to validate the name of your new folder.

Windows creates your new folder, which for now is empty.

# Managing files and folders

*Whatever you want to do with your folders or files (for example, to copy, move or delete one or more of them) you must start by selecting the folder(s) or file(s) concerned.*

## SELECTING FOLDERS AND FILES

▨ Open the folder window that contains the folders or files you want to select.

▨ If necessary, change the presentation of the file list using the [⊞▾] button and/or sort the file list using the **View - Arrange Icons by** command.

▨ To select several adjacent files in the list, point to an empty space just to the right of the first name you want to select then drag the mouse so that the dotted rectangle that appears surrounds the names and icons concerned then release the mouse button.

**Be careful: if the mouse pointer appears as a black circle with a diagonal bar across it and the file names move with the mouse pointer, release the mouse button immediately and start again.**

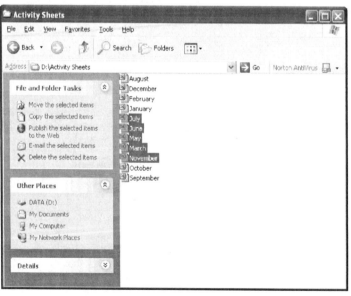

*Four files have been selected in this example.*

▨ To extend your selection of adjacent files to include other files further down the list, hold down the [Shift] key then click the document name you would like to appear at the end of the list.

**Windows XP**

For instance, if you want to include the **October** and **September** files in the example selection above, hold down the Shift key then click the **September** file name.

- To include another group of adjacent files or folders from the open folder (that is not adjacent to the existing group), hold down the Shift key then drag the mouse so that the dotted rectangle that appears surrounds the names and icons of the new group you want to include in your selection. When you are satisfied with your new selection, release the mouse button followed by the Shift key.

- To include another single file or folder from the open folder (that is not adjacent to the existing group), hold down the Ctrl key then click the name of the file or folder concerned.

  For instance, if you want to include the **August** file into the example selection above, hold down the Ctrl key then click the **August** file name.

- To select all the files and folders contained in the open folder, use the **Edit - Select All** command or press the Ctrl **A** key combination.

- To invert your selection, use the **Edit - Invert Selection** command.

 When you have selected a group of folders or files you can right-click your selection to view the menu options that you can apply to your selection (this is called a shortcut menu).

Once you have made your selection (be it a single file or a group), you can perform a variety of actions, such as deleting or copying the selected file(s).

*To select files, you must first access the folder that contains them. If you do not know the name of the folder that contains your files, you can search for your files in all the folders on your hard disk.*

## SEARCHING FOR FILES ACCORDING TO THEIR NAMES

- Click the **start** button on the taskbar then click the **Search** option.

  If a folder window is active, you can click the 🔎 Search tool button in this window to display the **Search Results** window.

※ If necessary, click the ▣ button in the **Search Results** window to display this window in full-screen mode and view all the options that the **Search Companion** offers.

By default, a little dog called **Rover** animates the **Search Companion** pane.

※ Click the **Documents (word processing, spreadsheet, etc.)** option.

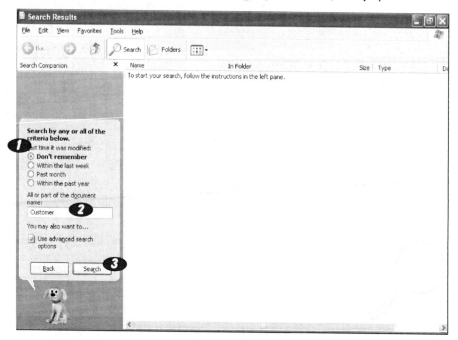

**1.** If you know when the file you seek was last modified, activate one of the three other options. Otherwise, leave the **Don't remember** option active.

**2.** Enter the name or part of the name of the document you seek. If you are not sure of the exact name of the document, you can use wildcard characters. Use the asterisk (*) to represent zero or more characters: (for example if you enter **cap***, you will find files called **cap, cape, caption, capture** and so forth). Use the question mark (?) to represent one character (for example, if you enter **cap?**, you will find the **cape** file but not the files **cap, caption, capture** and so forth).

**3.** Click to start the search.

**Windows XP**

When Windows has finished the search, it displays the items it has found in the right hand pane.

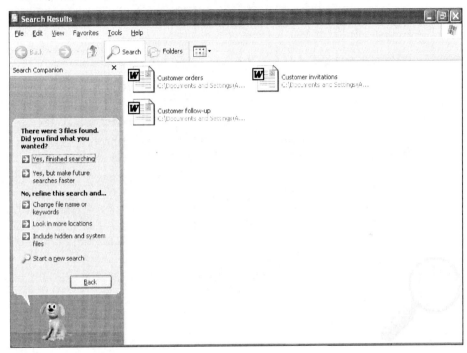

▨ To view a brief description of one of the files found, point to its name: a ScreenTip appears showing the file's type, author, size and so forth.

▨ To open one of these files, double-click its name (or its icon): the file opens along with the application that created it.

▨ To carry out another search, click the **Start a new search** link.

▨ To close the **Search Companion**, leaving the **Search Results** window open, click the **Yes, finished searching** link.

▨ To close the **Search Results** window, click the 🗙 button.

# Managing files and folders

*When you have created your folders, you can store appropriate files or folders in them. You can always copy these files into your new folders, but this approach will use more space than necessary and needlessly complicate your file management. It is generally a much better idea simply to move your folders and files from one folder to another.*

## MOVING FOLDERS AND FILES

- Click the **start** button then the **My Documents** option to open your personal folder window.

- Select the folder(s) or the file(s) you want to move.

- Under **File and Folder Tasks** in the left-hand pane of the window, click the **Move this folder** link or the **Move this file** link (if you selected only one folder or file) or the **Move the selected items** link (if you selected several folders and/or files).

- In the **Move Items** dialog box, click the name of the folder into which you want to move your folders or files. If this destination folder is not visible, click the + sign preceding the device name and/or the parent folder.

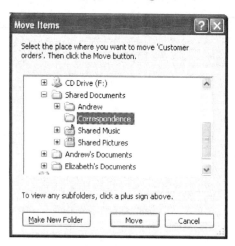

This example shows the **Customer orders** document being moved to the **Correspondence** subfolder of the **Shared Documents** folder.

- Click the **Move** button.

- If necessary, close the folder window.

 As its name suggests, the **Make New Folder** button in the **Move Items** dialog box creates a new destination folder.

**Windows XP**

*To duplicate a folder or a file, you can make a copy of it and, if you wish, rename the duplicate file.*

## COPYING FOLDERS AND FILES

▪ Click the **start** button then click the **My Documents** option to open your personal folder.

▪ In the left pane of the folder window, select the folder(s) or file(s) you want to copy.

▪ In the **File and Folder Tasks** box of the left pane, click the **Copy this file**, **Copy this folder** or **Copy the selected items** link, according to what you selected (if none of these options are visible, click the ⚲ button in the **File and Folder Tasks** box).

▪ In the **Copy Items** dialog box that appears, click the name of the folder into which you want to copy. If this destination folder is not visible in this dialog box, click the + sign preceding the name of the parent drive or folder.

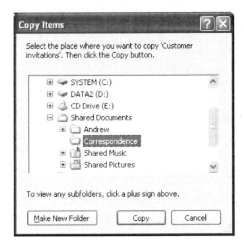

This example shows the **Customer invitations** file being copied into the **Correspondence** folder of the **Shared Documents** folder.

▪ Click the **Copy** button.

▪ If necessary, close the folder window.

 As its name suggests, the **Make New Folder** button on the **Copy Items** dialog box can create a new destination folder.
You can also copy folders or files in a folder window, by displaying the **Folders** explorer bar and using the **Copy** and **Paste** commands in the **Edit** menu.

# Managing files and folders

*You can duplicate a folder or file by copying it to a floppy disk. A floppy disk can be used to save your work, or to copy it elsewhere, or to give files to someone else.*

## COPYING FOLDERS OR FILES TO A FLOPPY DISK

▦ Check that your floppy disk drive contains a formatted floppy disk (cf. the Formatting a floppy disk section at the end of this chapter).

▦ Open the folder window that contains the folders or files you want to copy to your floppy disk.

▦ Select the folder(s) or the file(s) concerned.

▦ Use **File - Send To** then click the option corresponding to your floppy disk drive: this is often called **3$\frac{1}{2}$ Floppy (A)**.

A **Copying** window indicates how the copy is progressing. The noise of the floppy disk drive and its green light also indicate that the copy is underway.

 A standard floppy disk cannot contain more than 1.44 MB (1.44 Megabytes) or 1474 KB (1474 Kilobytes). If the file is too big, Windows displays a message to indicate that it is unable to copy it to the floppy disk.

*To tidy up your hard disk, you can delete files you no longer need. However, deleting a file by accident can cause hours or even days of extra work. To safeguard against such handling errors, Windows deletes your files in two stages: first, Windows moves these files to the Recycle Bin. The files no longer appear in your folder, but they are still present on your disk and you can recover them at any time. To remove your files permanently from your hard disk, you must delete them from the Recycle Bin.*

## DELETING FOLDERS AND FILES

▦ Click the **start** button then the **My Documents** option to open your personal folder window.

▦ Select the folder(s) or the file(s) you want to delete.

▦ Under **File and Folder Tasks,** click the **Delete this folder** link or the **Delete this file** link (if you selected only one folder or file) or the **Delete the selected items** link (if you selected several folders and/or files).

Alternatively, you can press the [Del] key or use the **File - Delete** command.

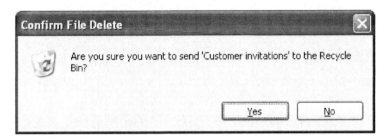

■ Click the **Yes** button to confirm that you want to send the folder(s) or file(s) to the Recycle Bin.

Almost immediately, the folder(s) or file(s) disappear from the folder window. **When you delete a folder, you also delete all the files and any subfolders it contains**.
This deletion is not final: the documents you have deleted are still present on the disk although they are no longer visible in your folder window.
To delete files permanently and free the disk space they occupy, you must either delete the files in the Recycle Bin or empty the Recycle Bin.
**Important note**: if you delete items from a drive other than your computer's hard disk (for example, from a floppy disk or from a drive on the network) Windows does not use the Recycle Bin and you will not be able to recover these files later.

If the files you want to delete are contained in **several folders**, you can run a search for them then select them in the **Search Results** window before deleting them.

To delete a file permanently from your disk without using the Recycle Bin, select it and press the ⌈Shift⌉⌈Del⌉ keys instead of the ⌈Del⌉ key alone. Do not use this key combination unless you are absolutely sure that you no longer need the files you have selected.

# Managing files and folders

*When you have deleted a file you can still view it in, and recover it from, a special folder called the **Recycle Bin**.*

## MANAGING FOLDERS AND FILES IN THE RECYCLE BIN

▦ To view files you have deleted, double-click the **Recycle Bin** icon on your desktop to open this folder.

The folders and files contained in the Recycle Bin appear. You can manage this list as you would manage the list of items in any other folder: use the options of the **View** menu to define its presentation.

▦ To recover one or more files or folders from the Recycle Bin, select the items concerned in this window then, under **Recycle Bin Tasks**, click the **Restore this item** link (if you selected only one folder or file) or the **Restore the selected items** link (if you selected several folders and/or files).

The files and/or folders disappear from the Recycle Bin. Windows restores each item to the folder from which it was deleted, recreating this folder if it no longer exists.

▦ To restore all the items in the Recycle Bin to the folders from which they were deleted, make sure that no folder or file is selected and click the **Restore all items** link under **Recycle Bin Tasks**.

- To delete permanently one or more folders and/or files and thereby free the disk space that they occupy, select the folders and/or files in the Recycle Bin window then select **File - Delete** or press the ⌞Del⌟ key. Confirm your action by clicking the **Yes** button.

- To delete permanently all the folders and files in the Recycle Bin, click the **Empty the Recycle Bin** link under **Recycle Bin Tasks**. Confirm your action by clicking the **Yes** button.

  After you have emptied your Recycle Bin, it will remain empty until you delete other folders or files.

 To delete permanently all the folders and files in the Recycle Bin, you can also right-click the **Recycle Bin** icon on your desktop and choose the **Empty Recycle Bin** option.

*Although most commercially available floppy disks are preformatted, you may sometimes need to format or to reformat a floppy disk. This operation allows your operating system to organise the floppy disk according to the characteristics of your computer's floppy-disk drive (in particular, it determines the capacity of the floppy disk).*

## FORMATTING A FLOPPY DISK

- Insert the floppy disk in your floppy-disk drive.
- Open the **My Computer** window using the **start - My Computer** command.
- Right-click the icon for your floppy-disk drive, which is often called **3₁/₂ Floppy (A:)**.
- Click the **Format** option.

# Managing files and folders

*The capacity of the floppy disk is expressed in Megabytes (MB) or in Kilobytes (KB)*
*Remember that a byte is the space required to store one character.*
*The information 3.5" refers to the physical dimension of the floppy disk.*

*1.* If necessary, define the **Capacity** of the floppy disk according to its physical characteristics. For a High Density floppy disk, choose **1.44 MB**; for a Low Density floppy disk, choose **720 KB** (most modern floppy disks are High Density disks).

*2.* If required, specify the name you want to give your floppy disk. This name cannot be longer than 11 characters (for FAT file systems).

*3.* If your floppy disk has already been formatted, activate the **Quick Format** option to allow Windows to delete the contents of the floppy disk, without checking the sectors on the disk. However, if you re-format the disk often, you should regularly use the complete formatting technique to test the disk's viability.

*4.* Click the **Start** button to start formatting.

Windows XP

A message appears to warn you that the formatting operation will delete all the files on your floppy disk.

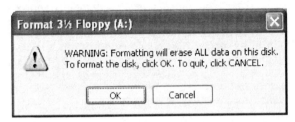

▪ Click the **OK** button to confirm that you want to format your floppy disk.

▪ At the end of the operation, click the **OK** button on the message informing you that the formatting is complete.

▪ Click the **Close** button in the **Format 3 1/2 Floppy (A:)** dialog box.

If you try to use a floppy disk that has not been formatted, Windows will display an error message indicating that the floppy disk has not been formatted and offering to do it for you.

If Windows tells you at the end of formatting that the floppy disk contains bad (or defective) sectors, it would a good idea to throw out the floppy. Even though the system will not write data on any of the defective parts, it is a sign that the floppy is probably not reliable.

# Installing

*If your computer came with a printer, you must install this device physically by connecting it to your computer via a cable, according to the manufacturer's instructions. When you run a print command, Windows sends instructions to the printer. However, each printer needs specific instructions that it can understand. For the printer to be able to understand the instructions Windows sends, your hard disk must contain a special file, called a driver. This driver provides a link between Windows and the printer. The Windows XP CD-ROM contains a large number of drivers and it probably includes one for your printer. However, if the Windows XP CD-ROM does not provide a driver for your printer, you will find one on the CD-ROM or floppy disk supplied with your printer.*

## INSTALLING A PRINTER

▓ Click the **start** button followed by the **Control Panel** option.

▓ In Category view, click the **Printers and Other Hardware** link followed by the **Add a printer** link.

The **Add Printer Wizard** starts.

▓ Click the **Next** button.

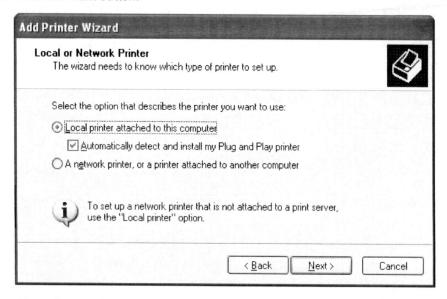

▓ If you have only one computer, activate the **Local printer attached to this computer** option. If you leave the **Automatically detect and install my Plug and Play printer** option active, Windows may be able to detect your newly connected printer and install it automatically.

**Windows XP**

If your computer is part of a network and the printer is connected to another machine in the network, activate the **A network printer, or a printer attached to another computer** option.

- Click the **Next** button.

- If you are installing a network printer, leave the **Browse for a printer** option active, click the **Next** button then select one of the printers in the **Shared printers** list and click the **Next** button.

- If you are installing a local printer and the **Automatically detect and install my Plug and Play printer** option was not active in the previous screen, you can change the output port in the **Use the following port** list, if it does not correspond to the port to which you connected your printer. Click the **Next** button.

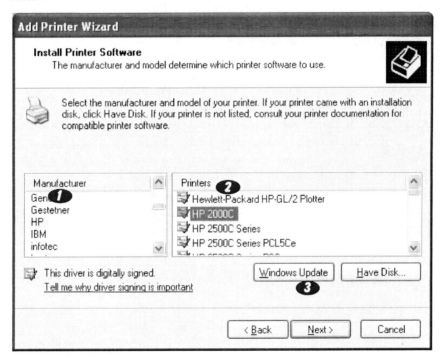

*1.* Select the make of your printer.

**2.** Select your printer model: if the exact model of your printer is not in the list, select the nearest model or insert the CD-ROM or floppy disk that contains the driver into your computer then click the **Have Disk** button. Check that the correct drive is selected in the **Copy manufacturer's files from** list then click the **OK** button and select the name of your printer.

**3.** Continue with the installation procedure.

- If you are installing a local printer, specify the **Printer name** in the corresponding box, if necessary.

- Specify whether or not Windows applications must use the printer by default then click the **Next** button.

- Specify whether or not you want to print a test page (printing a test page is a good idea as it allows you to check that your printer is working properly) then click the **Next** button.

- Click the **Finish** button.

- Click the ▨ button on the **Printers and Faxes** window to close it.

To install hardware devices on your computer such as scanners, printers or digital cameras, start the **Add Hardware Wizard**. Select **start - Control Panel - Printers and Other Hardware - Add Hardware** link (in the **See Also** box) then follow the installation procedure.

It is much simpler to install a **USB** device: just connect the device to one of the USB ports of your computer (you do not even need to switch your computer off to do this) and the installation procedure runs automatically. Follow the installation steps.

**Windows XP**

*There are two reasons why you might want to install an external screen; the inbuilt screen on your laptop may be too small or of poor quality and you are not comfortable working with it, or you want to display two different things, one on either screen. A multi-screen display is something that more recent models offers, as older style laptops could handle multiple screens, but could not display a different item on each screen (the same view appeared on each one).*

## INSTALLING AN EXTERNAL SCREEN

Most laptops have a socket into which you can plug a second screen.

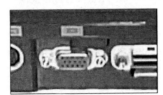

You can manage this second screen through the display settings.

▨ Click the **start** menu then **ControlPanel**. Click the **Display** icon (you might not see this icon, if your Control Panel is displayed in Category view; if so, click the **Appearance and Themes** link to see the **Display** icon).

The **Display Properties** dialog box opens.

▨ Click the **Settings** tab to see the screen settings.

▨ If you have already plugged in the second screen and if you have the appropriate video card on your computer, the dialog box lets you set up each screen independently, as shown below.

▨ You can choose a different resolution (the number of dots and lines displayed) for each screen. If you don't know how Windows has numbered the screens, click the **Identify** button; Windows displays a large number on each screen, corresponding to the number in the dialog box.

If you don't see these options, this means that your computer's video card cannot handle two screens.

The options open to you vary depending on the video card installed and the drivers that come with it. You could display different windows and/or applications on each screen or spread your desktop over two screens, etc. For example, the **Extend my Windows desktop onto this monitor** option spills the desktop (the screen area in which you can display application windows) over onto the second screen, giving you double the display area. When you push the pointer out of the first screen, it appears automatically on the second one. You can also move windows from one screen to another by dragging them over. One piece of advice: always read your laptop's user manual before investing in a second screen, to be sure of what you can use and how you can use it!

*After you have bought a software application on a CD-ROM or a floppy disk, you must install it on your hard disk before you can use it (installing an application consists of copying the application files onto your hard disk and defining settings to make the application work). You would generally carry out this operation using an installation wizard, which asks you certain questions as the installation progresses (such as on which drive you want to install your application and whether you want to install the full version or a limited one).*

## INSTALLING A PROGRAM (APPLICATION)

You need to use a Computer administrator type of account to install some programs.

▨ If your application is on a CD-ROM, insert the CD-ROM in your computer's CD-ROM drive.

Most applications on CD-ROM offer an Autorun or setup feature, which installs the application automatically.

▨ In this case, click the **Install** button to start the installation process and follow the instructions that appear on the screen (these instructions vary from one application to another).

▨ If your application does not install itself automatically (or if your application is on a floppy disk) access the **Control Panel** (**start - Control Panel**) then (in Category view) click the **Add or Remove Programs** link.

Your laptop

A list of the applications currently installed on your hard disk appears in this dialog box:

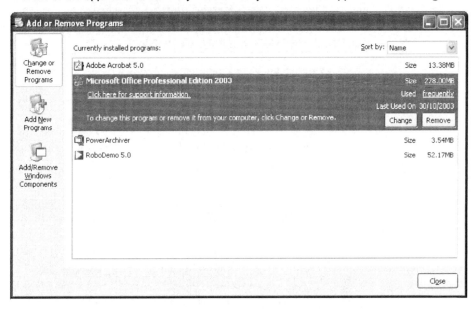

■ Click the **Add New Programs** button followed by the **CD or Floppy** button.

■ Insert the application's CD-ROM or first floppy disk in the appropriate drive of your computer, as Windows asks you to, then click the **Next** button.

Windows searches your CD-ROM or floppy disk for the application's installation program then displays its name in the **Open** box. You can use the **Browse** button to look for your installation program manually.

■ Click the **Finish** button to start the installation procedure.

Windows copies the files it needs to install the application.

■ Follow the different steps of the installation program, until the end.

When you have installed an application, its name appears in the **start** - **All Programs** menu, which is common to all the users of the computer. You can run your application from this menu.

# Installing

*When you no longer need an application it is a good idea to uninstall it. Rather than simply deleting the folder that contains the application's files, you are strongly advised to follow the uninstall procedure set out below.*

## UNINSTALLING A PROGRAM (APPLICATION)

Before you attempt to uninstall a program, you may need to logon with a Computer administrator type account.

▨ Access the **Control Panel** from the **start** menu.

▨ Click the **Add or Remove Programs** link (in Category view).

▨ Click the **Change or Remove Programs** button in the left of the window.

▨ In the **Currently installed programs** list, click the row corresponding to the program you want to remove.

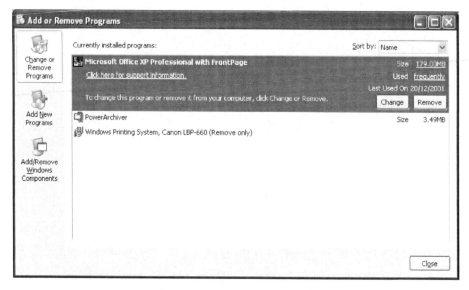

According to the application concerned, Windows may provide a **Change** button and a **Remove** button or a single **Change/Remove** button.

▨ Click the **Remove** button or the **Change/Remove** button.

Windows asks you to confirm your action.

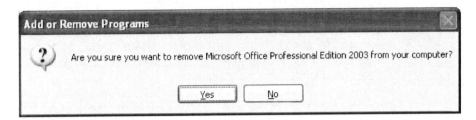

- Click the **Yes** button.

  Windows removes all the application files you no longer need.

- When Windows has finished the uninstall procedure, click the **OK** button.

- Click the **Close** button in the **Add or Remove Programs** dialog box.

- Click the ⊠ button to close the **Control Panel**.

# The Briefcase

## WHAT IS THE BRIEFCASE USED FOR?

When you are in the office, you are probably connected to a server on your company network. A server is an especially powerful computer used to store shared data such as programs, documents and other data. Depending on how the work is organized on your company's network, you will probably find that often you are working with documents that are not actually stored on your portable computer, but on a server.

Of course, once you disconnect your computer and take it out of the office, this type of data is no longer available to you.

One way of solving this problem is to copy the files onto your computer before you leave the office. This is a satisfactory solution providing that you know how to organize your files and that there are not too many of them (as seen in the Managing files and folders chapter).

Windows also provides you with a tool called the Briefcase, which gives you a practical solution to this kind of problem. You take the files away, in a special folder on your laptop (the briefcase in question), use them, and then synchronize the files when you get back to the office.

## USING THE BRIEFCASE

▦ Right-click the desktop (or right-click any Windows Explorer window) and point to the **New** option then click **Briefcase**

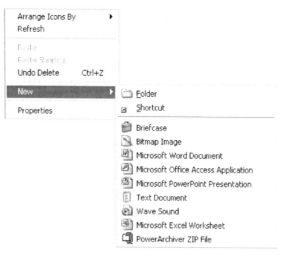

Windows creates a folder called **New Briefcase**.

▨ Double-click the briefcase's icon to open it.

▨ When the briefcase opens, a dialog box appears to give you information on how to use it.

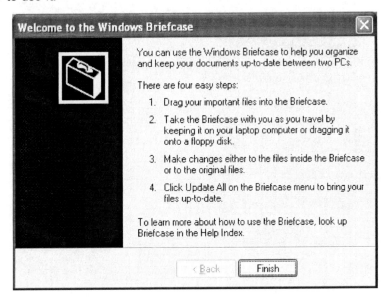

▨ Click the **Finish** button.

▨ Drag the documents you want to take away into the briefcase window.

# The Briefcase

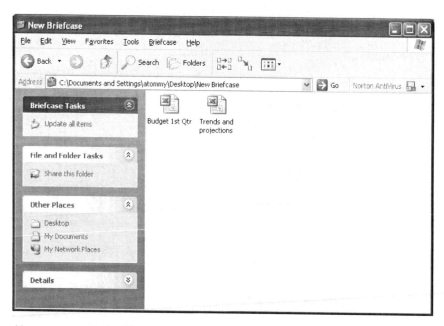

- You can now turn off your computer and leave the office.

- When you want to work on the documents at home (or somewhere else), simply use them directly from the briefcase window.

- Once you get back to the office, connect your portable computer to the network again and use one of the synchronization buttons on the toolbar:

    to make a complete update of all the files.

    to update only the selected files (select them with the mouse first).

In this example, one of the documents has been deleted from the briefcase and another has been modified. Windows offers to update the original files.

▓ Click the **Update** button.

In this example, the document called **Budget 1$^{st}$ Qtr** on disk D: will be replaced by the one in the Briefcase. The document **Trends and Projections** will be deleted from disk D.

*Windows XP offers several multimedia applications, such as the Windows Media Player, which you can use for playing audio CDs, watching DVDs and so on. Internet technology plays such an important role in our daily lives; you can use your computer to discover a new world of information, via the "global village".*

# 5th Part

# Multimedia and communication

**5.1 Windows Media Player**      p.144

**5.2 Getting started on the Internet**      p.154

**5.3 Working with the browser**      p.158

**5.4 E-mail**      p.162

# Windows Media Player

*The Microsoft Windows Media Player can read a large number of audio and video file formats from your computer or from the Internet. You can use the Windows Media Player to listen to radio stations from anywhere in the world, read and copy CDs, read DVDs (if you have a DVD drive) or look for available videos on the Internet. It will even manage customized lists of all the digital multimedia files stored on your computer. This chapter describes the* **9 series** *version of Windows Media Player.*

## DISCOVERING THE WINDOWS MEDIA PLAYER

※ To open this application, click the **start** button then **All Programs - Windows Media Player**.

※ The **Windows Media Player** window contains:
- a title bar and menus (a): this area appears automatically when you point to the **Playlist Selection** area (b). To keep this bar on the screen or make it disappear again, click the ⊚ button on the **Playlist Selection** area.
- the player display area (c).
- the **Playlist Selection** area (d): you can use the buttons in this area to choose a playlist or another type of element or to display play and playlist tools.

Multimedia and communication

- the **Features Taskbar** (e): this bar contains seven or eight buttons; each button runs a specific feature (you can also access these features using the **View - Taskbar** menu option).
- the **Playback Controls** (f) area.

▨ If your Internet connection is open when you start the **Windows Media Player**, it will display the contents of the WindowsMedia.com site in its monitor automatically. If you have an on-demand connection (via a modem for example) click the **Media Guide** button then confirm your request to access the network to obtain the guide's contents. If you do not request a connection, the reader display area stays black.

▨ Select **View - Skin Mode** or [Ctrl] **2** or [🔲] to give your **Media Player** a skin appearance and select **View - Full Mode** or [Ctrl] **1** or double-click [🔲] to restore your **Media Player** to its normal appearance.

*When you play an audio CD, **Windows Media Player** provides an attractive interface, including an effect called a visualization, whose look you can alter to suit your taste.*

## PLAYING AN AUDIO CD

▨ If it is closed, open the **Windows Media Player** application (**start - All Programs - Windows Media Player**) then insert an audio CD in your CD-ROM drive.

If you insert an audio CD before starting the **Windows Media Player** application, Windows XP may show you this window:

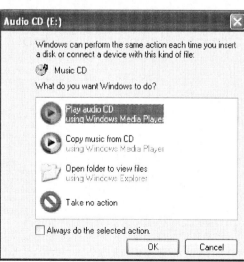

# Windows Media Player

⊞ If this happens, click the **Play Audio CD using Windows Media Player** option and click **OK**; this will activate the Windows Media Player and start playing the CD.

If the Windows Media Player does not recognize your CD, it will show "Artist Unknown".

⊞ If necessary, click the **Now Playing** button on the **Features Taskbar**.

⊞ In the **Playlist** pane, click the required track then click the ⊙ button on the **Playback Controls** area to start playing the track (once you activate it, this button changes into ⊙).

⊞ Use these commands to manage the playback options:

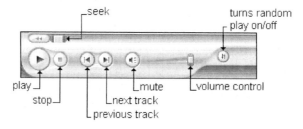

The track currently playing appears in green in the **Playlist** pane and the length already played is shown at the bottom right of the window.

To change the visualization that appears in the centre of the player in the **Now Playing** page, use the **View - Visualizations** command on the menu bar then activate the required view.

You can also click the ▦ button at the bottom left of the player and choose one of the options offered. There are not as many options here as in the **Visualizations** menu.

*You can listen to some national and international radio stations over the Internet: a continuous broadcasting process makes this possible. For the user, the main advantage of this is that he or she can listen to the radio without waiting for sound files to be loaded, avoiding a "chopped" sound effect. To carry out the following actions, your Internet connection must be open.*

## LISTENING TO THE RADIO

### Looking at the Radio Tuner

▦ If it is closed, open the **Windows Media Player** application (**start** - **All Programs - Windows Media Player**).

▦ Click the **Radio Tuner** button on the **Features Taskbar**.

By default, the Windows Media Player displays the radio information available on the WindowsMedia.com web site:

# Windows Media Player

The Player window shows links to radio stations, classified into three categories: **Featured Stations, My Stations** and **Recently Played Stations**.

- To show or hide the contents on any of these categories, click the corresponding 🔘 button.

## Finding a radio station

- Click the **Radio Tuner** button on the **Features Taskbar**.
- To make a station search, click one of the required radio types located in the right pane of the screen, or enter in the appropriate text box a keyword representing the station you want to find. If you enter a keyword, finish by clicking the 🔘 button.

WindowsMedia.com lists the stations that correspond to your search and also allows you to qualify your search request with more criteria:

- To make a combined search using a genre and a keyword, fill in the **Browse by Genre** box and the **Search** box then click the 🔘 button to the right of the **Search** box, to start the search.

The **Zip Code** search criterion is valid only in the USA.

- To return to the previous page, click the **Return to My Stations** link.

## Listening to a radio station

- Click the **RadioTuner** button on the **FeaturesTaskbar**.
- If the radio station to which you want to listen is not in any of the three categories offered, make a search to view it (cf. Finding a radio station, above).

▓ Click the link corresponding to the radio station concerned, to see some details about it.

| Station Name ▲ | Speed | Location |
|---|---|---|
| ▷ 101 FM | 28K | Leavenwo |
| ▷ 101.6 FM All That Jazz with Brian Parker | 56K | Net Only |
| ▷ AccuHolidays: Holiday Jazz | 56K | Net Only |
| ▷ AccuRadio - All That Jazz | 56K | Net Only |

Search Results: Jazz

56K : Jazz : Net Only
Explore the art of improvisation with masters such as Miles Davis, J
Thelonious Monk
+ Add to My Stations | 🖵 Visit Website to Play

| ▷ AccuRadio - All That Jazz: Guitar Jazz | 56K | Net Only |
|---|---|---|
| ▷ AccuRadio - All That Jazz: Piano Jazz | 56K | Net Only |

▓ Click the **Visit Website to Play** button to listen to the selected station.

You can also listen to a station by clicking the [▷] button just to the left of its name.

Note that each time you start listening to a radio station, your PC's Web browser (such as Internet Explorer) opens and displays the active station's home page: additional advertising screens, called pop-ups may also appear. You can quickly get swamped by these! If you wish to see or close a pop-up, you may first have to activate it by clicking its button on the taskbar.

▓ To stop the radio, click the [■] button in the **Playback Controls** area in the **Windows Media Player** window, if you have been playing the radio directly from Media Player; if you have been playing it directly from the radio web site, close the appropriate window or click the window's "Stop" button.

# Windows Media Player

## MEDIA PLAYER AND DVDS

### Playing a DVD

▓ Insert the DVD in the DVD drive.

Windows Media Player may start automatically. However, if your computer has several DVD playing applications and the Media Player window is not open, the following dialog box appears so that you can choose the application you want to use:

▓ Click the **Play DVD Video using Windows Media Player** option.

The contents of the DVD appear in the Playlist pane. In the example above, the DVD contains several titles and each title contains one or more chapters.

- To view the chapters for a title, click the + sign to the left of the title concerned. To hide the chapters for a title, click the - sign to the left of the title concerned.

- To play a DVD manually, open the **Play** menu and use the **DVD or CD Audio** command, or open the list in the top right corner and click the name of the DVD you want to play.

- In the Playlist pane, click the title or chapter of the DVD you want to play.

- To view your DVD in full screen mode, select the **View - Full Screen** command or press [Alt] [Enter] or click the ▦ button.

When you switch to full screen view, the Player controls appear briefly then disappear.

# Windows Media Player

These items disappear automatically from the screen after a few moments.

▓ To restore these controls to the screen, move your mouse or press any key.

 Before you start playing a DVD, it is advisable to deactivate the screen saver. Select the **Tools - Options - Player** tab then deactivate the **Allow screen saver during playback** option.
To specify any **Parental control** or **Language settings**, select **Tools - Options - DVD** tab and choose the required options.

### Capturing a still picture from a DVD

▓ Play the DVD concerned.

▓ **View - DVD Features - Image Capture**

The **Image Capture** command will be available only if your graphics card and your DVD decoder support this feature.

▓ If necessary, select the folder in which you want to save the image then enter the **File name**.

▓ If necessary, change the **Save as type** option.

▓ Click the **Save** button.

*You can change the look of your Windows Media Player by applying different "skins" (or presentations) to it.*

### CHANGING THE LOOK OF THE WINDOWS MEDIA PLAYER

▓ If it is closed, open the **Windows Media Player** application (**start** - **All Programs** - **Windows Media Player**).

▓ Click the **Skin Chooser** button on the **Features Taskbar**.

Multimedia and communication

**1.** Click one of the skins offered: a preview of your selected skin appears in the right part of the window.

**2.** To apply the selected skin to the Windows Media Player, click the **Apply Skin** button.

The Windows Media Player takes on the selected appearance.

▧ To return to **Full Mode** view, double-click the ⬚ symbol or press `Ctrl` **1**.

▧ To adopt the **Skin Mode** again, click the ⬚ button or choose the **Skin Mode** option in the **View** menu or press `Ctrl` **2**.

To download other skins from the WindowsMedia.com site, click the **More Skins** button (your Internet connection must be open) then download one of the skins on offer by clicking the appropriate link.

# Getting started on the Internet

*Although the Internet is made up of complicated technologies, you do not need to understand them before you can use it. Below you will find all the information you need to get started.*

## ACCESSING THE INTERNET

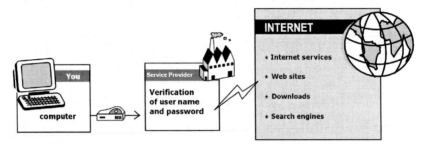

This diagram illustrates the principle of Internet access for home users.

- To access the Internet, you will need a contract with a service provider. You will also need a modem for your computer, which will communicate with the service provider, or, more precisely, with the service provider's computer.
- The service provider's computer will ask for your username, or login, and your password. If these are correct, you will then be able to use the Internet.
- Here is what you need to connect to the Internet:
    - a connection method and an appropriate modem for this method,
    - a contract with an Internet Service Provider (ISP) (a CD-ROM for subscribing to an ISP may have been supplied with your computer),
    - a computer with a modem that has been configured to know which ISP it must contact.

*When you have looked at all the different connection options and chosen your ISP, you will be ready to install everything you need to connect.*

## THE DIFFERENT STEPS TO CONNECTION

### 1 - Installing your modem

- If the modem is not already installed, you will need to install it. Refer to the instructions for physically installing the modem then to those for installing the necessary driver (this is a file that will enable the modem to communicate with your computer's operating system).

- Before you start to install your connection kit, it is a good idea to check that your modem is correctly installed:
    - Click **start - Control Panel - Printers and Other Hardware - Phone and Modem Options - Modems** tab.
    - If you can see your modem in the modem list with the correct name then your modem is installed correctly.
- If there is a problem, refer to the manual you received with the modem to find the correct configuration, or contact the hardware supplier. Your ISP helpline will probably be able to resolve minor problems.

## 2 - Contacting your chosen ISP

- First, contact the ISP to subscribe to the service.
- Your ISP will supply the information you will need to connect to the Internet:
    - your username or login,
    - your password,
    - your e-mail address.

Your ISP will also supply more technical information such as:

- the name of the POP server,
- the name of the SMTP server,
- the name of the news server,
- the telephone number for the ISP's server.
- You should also receive a connection kit (a CD-ROM) including a program that will install your connection and the necessary software automatically.

Some connection kits allow you to subscribe to an ISP, without having first contacted the provider.

### 3 - Installing the connection kit

- The CD-ROM should run automatically, but if it does not, follow the instructions it provides.

- The program provided by your ISP will install a number of applications automatically:

  - a browser (Internet Explorer or Netscape Navigator),

  - an e-mail and news program (such as Outlook Express or Netscape Messenger).

  **If any of these applications is already present on your computer, you can still install the ISP's programs. If the version you have is older than that of the ISP, it will be updated or if you have the same version, the ISP's application will replace it.**

- The program will configure these applications (by defining settings such as the names of the POP and SMTP servers) and configure your Internet connection. You will need to give some information, such as:

  - your username,

  - your password,

  - your e-mail address.

- If you have chosen AOL as your ISP, the applications provided will be specific to AOL. If you have any questions, you will need to call the AOL helpline.

 **If you are using only one ISP, your computer will connect to this provider automatically when you launch your browser. However, you can choose to install several connections if you want to use more than one ISP to access the Internet.**

**Multimedia and communication**

*Internet, the Web, e-mail, discussion groups... what does it all mean?*

## UNDERSTANDING THE DIFFERENT USES OF THE INTERNET

▨ The term Internet simply describes the network (the wires, basically) that enables you to access the services.

▨ The most frequently used services are:

- e-mail,
- searches for information,
- file transfers (downloading software, images, videos, music and so on),
- themed discussion groups.

▨ Other services include online chat, telephony and webcams.

**These services all use the Internet network, but are independent of each other. You can access each of them via a specific protocol and a specific application.**

# Working with the browser

*Along with e-mail, the Web is the most popular service that the Internet offers, so much so that the two terms are commonly confused. However, the Web is in fact only a part of the Internet. You can access it via a browser.*

## UNDERSTANDING THE WEB AND THE ROLE OF BROWSERS

▓ The Web, or World Wide Web, is a collection of over a billion pages that contain mostly text, images, graphics and photos. It is growing all the time. These web pages are generally contained on sites, maintained by companies, organisations or domains.

▓ Your browser lets you see the content of these pages. When you installed your Internet connection, your browser was configured either automatically or manually.

▓ The most popular browsers are Internet Explorer and Netscape Navigator. The former is installed automatically on your PC with Windows XP (or Windows 2000). The latter is included in the Netscape Communicator suite. Both programs are freely available for download from the Microsoft site (http://www.microsoft.com) or the Netscape site (http://www.netscape.com).

*To access a Web site you must first start your browser so that it appears on the screen.*

## STARTING YOUR BROWSER

▓ Click the **start** button on the taskbar at the bottom of the Windows desktop then drag the mouse pointer to the **Internet** option and click.

The application (your browser software) appears in a window. If you are not already connected to the Internet, the dial-up connection process will start automatically. Let the modem call your ISP, who will verify your username and password.

*The Microsoft Internet Explorer 6 window.*

What you see on your screen may not correspond exactly to what is shown in these illustrations. Nevertheless, it is important to pick out the basic tools in your browser.

**a.** The menu bar.

**b.** This icon might be that of Netscape, Internet Explorer, or your ISP.

**c.** The address bar.

**d.** The web page display.

*Below you can learn how to use these essential tools. They were created in Illinois in 1993 by the creators of Mosaic, the first browser, and are so efficient that all current browsers use them. This means that if you change from one browser to another, you will never be completely lost.*

## DISPLAYING YOUR FIRST WEB PAGE

▨ Click in the text box on the address bar (c).

▨ Delete the text that is there and replace it with the address of the site you want to visit. For example, type **http://www.eni-publishing.com**.

# Working with the browser

When you type a Web address, remember:

- not to use apostrophes,

- not to use spaces,

- that the only characters allowed (apart from letters and numbers) are the forward slash (/), hyphens (-), underscores (_) and full stops (.).

▨ Confirm by pressing Enter.

The (b) icon begins to turn and the status bar indicates how close the page is to loading.

▨ When the icon stops turning and the status bar reads **Done** or **Document: Done**, the page you wanted is fully displayed in the window (d) (if you typed the address of a site, the site's homepage is shown).

 If you cannot see all of the page contents, use the scroll bars to the right and at the bottom of the window to discover the entire page.
If the page takes too long to display and you lose patience, click the **Stop** button to stop the page from loading, then try another address.

The Web uses a hyperlink system, in which you go from one page to another by clicking hyperlinks. In each page you will find one or more links. When you activate a link, it starts loading another page, in which you will find yet more hyperlinks.

## ACTIVATING HYPERLINKS IN A PAGE

▨ To find where the links are in a page, move the mouse pointer around. When the pointer takes the shape of a hand, it is over a link.

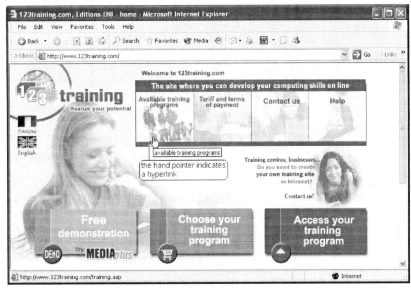

*A link might take the form of certain words in the text or of an image.*
*When you point to a link, the address of the page to which itleads appears*
*on the status bar at he bottom of the window.*

Traditionally, text that is associated with a link appears in blue and is underlined, but fewer and fewer web pages respect this convention as designers place more importance on the aspect of their pages. The best way to find links is to move the mouse pointer all around the page, not forgetting to use the scroll bars, of course!

To activate a link and display a new page, click the link in question.

Some links go from page to page within the same site, in which case the beginning of the address (the site or server's address) stays the same:

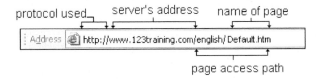

Other links will send you to a different site and you will notice a change in the appearance of the pages and a different address in the browser's address bar.

**Happy surfing!**

# E-mail

Multimedia and communication

*Along with the Web browser, e-mail is one of the most popular services that the Internet provides. You can send your e-mail messages to other people who have an Internet connection, in only a few moments. When you send a message it first goes to a computer called an outgoing mail server, which reads your recipient's address and sends it on in the right direction. Conversely, when you receive a message, your incoming mail server stores it for you. Your ISP manages these servers and provides your mailbox at your e-mail address (do not confuse e-mail addresses with web page addresses).*

## E-MAIL ADDRESSES

▨ You can recognise e-mail addresses because they contain the @ character.

▨ An e-mail address takes this form: user_name@server_name.

| | |
|---|---|
| **user_name** | this is the name or assumed name of the address' owner. It is often created using the first name (or initial) and surname of the person, which are sometimes separated with a hyphen or full stop. For example:<br>anne.watson@server_name<br>awatson@server_name<br>However, there are many variants! |
| @ | a special character known as **at**. |
| **server_name** | this identifies the computer that stores the mailbox. |

▨ The server's name will depend on what sort of e-mail you have:

- Mailbox with your ISP:
  anne.watson@serviceprovider.co.uk

- Mailbox at your workplace:
  anne.watson@company.co.uk

- Web-based mailbox (e-mail that you access by logging on to a web site, offered by several sites such as Yahoo!, Hotmail.com, Lycos.co.uk):
  annewatson@yahoo.co.uk

This last type of e-mail is convenient if you are often on the move, because you can use it to check your e-mail from any computer.

*All e-mail applications provide the same basic features. Only if you are using a Web-based mailbox will you have to get used to something a little different.*

## GETTING TO KNOW YOUR E-MAIL SOFTWARE

▨ First find the following in your program (or Web-based mailbox):

  **a.** Inbox.

  **b.** Messages you have sent.

  **c.** Messages that are ready to be sent.

  **d.** Draft messages.

  **e.** Waste bin (or trash).

▨ In **Outlook Express**:

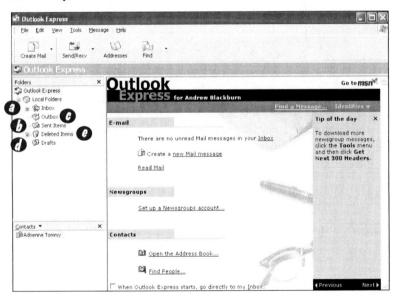

*The techniques detailed in this section are based on the Outlook Express e-mail program. Nevertheless, you should not have any trouble finding the equivalent commands in other e-mail software and Web-based e-mail.*

## SENDING A MESSAGE

Before you can do this, your e-mail program needs to be correctly configured, which means that it needs to know the names of your incoming and outgoing mail servers, your e-mail address, and your name.

Open your e-mail program.

**Message - New Message** or 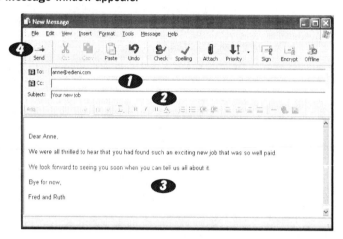 or `Ctrl` **N**

A **New Message** window appears.

1. Type the recipient's address carefully: unlike postmen, computers can deliver messages only if the address has been typed correctly. If you are sending the message to several people, separate the addresses with semi-colons.

2. Type in a few words to give the message a subject. This should resume the message contents and is important, because many people manage their incoming messages according to the subject.

3. Enter the text of the message here. You can write as much as you like.

4. Click this button to send the message.

   Once the message has been sent, it appears in the sent messages box.

 It is a good idea to prepare all your messages offline. You should connect to the Internet only to send and receive messages, as this will keep your connection times short.

**Multimedia and communication**

*As this chapter described previously, you will need to ask your server to send your new e-mail messages to your computer before you can read them.*

## COLLECTING YOUR MAIL

▩ Click the [Send/Recv] button.

This command will copy your messages onto your hard drive. You can disconnect as soon as you have finished.

▩ Now open the new mail folder, the **Inbox**.

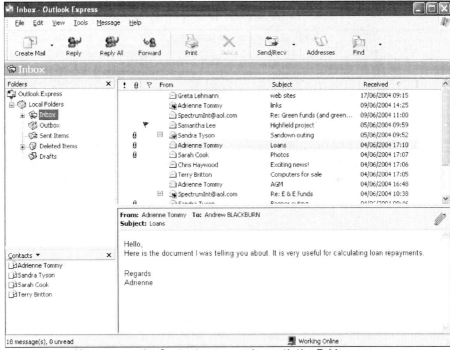

You can see the **Contacts** pane underneath the **Folders** pane.

▩ Double-click a message to read its contents.

The message appears in a new window.

*In addition to text, you can attach documents to your messages (such as pictures, graphs and spreadsheets). For example, imagine that you are planning a family party and you want to send your menu ideas to your sister, who lives at the other end of the country. You can type out your ideas in Word (for example), then send them to your sister, who can make any changes she might think appropriate. Once she has made her changes, she can return the Word file to you by e-mail, along with a list of all the guests in an Excel file. These documents are sent as attachments to the e-mails.*

## ATTACHED FILES (ATTACHMENTS)

- Write the message as described above.
- Use the **Insert - File Attachment** command in Outlook Express.
- Select the file you want to attach to the message then click **Open** or **Attach**.
- Repeat these steps if you want to attach more files.
- Now send the message.

When you receive an attached file, a paper clip appears next to the message. Open the message and double-click the attachment icon. The e-mail application then asks you if you want to open or to save the file. Be careful here, as attachments often carry viruses (a virus is a program that destroys or damages files on your disk). Installing an anti-virus program on your computer is an excellent idea, but may not be enough: new viruses appear every day. For effective protection you must update your anti-virus program regularly, either automatically using a subscription or manually from the Internet.

However, you can limit considerably the risk of catching a virus, simply by not opening e-mails you receive from unknown sources.

You have no doubt realised that Windows has to work hard to juggle between the system, all the open applications and the (sometimes dubious!) actions that we carry out. It is little wonder that sometimes things go wrong! This last section shows you some of the more common error messages that you may see and the various problems that can occur, with a few troubleshooting tips.

# Part

# Troubleshooting

## 6.1 **Technical problems**     p.168

# Technical problems

*When you start Windows, it begins by scrolling comments on black screens before showing the desktop. Sometimes, however, unexpected problems may occur.*

## FLOPPY DISK

- You may see the following message:

  **Non-system disk or disk error**

  **Replace and strike any key when ready**

- When Windows starts up, it tries to read specific files that contain information on the hardware and its general configuration. This message indicates that your computer was unable to find these files.

  - In most cases, this message means that there is a disk in the floppy disk drive. If you remove this floppy disk then press any key, Windows should be able to start normally.

  - If this is not the case, these files have probably been deleted, damaged or moved: consult your computer dealer or a person who has in-depth knowledge of your operating system.

*You want to access a drive (such as a floppy, zip or CD-ROM drive) but Windows will not let you do so.*

## DRIVE INACCESSIBLE

- Windows shows a message telling you that it cannot read this drive:

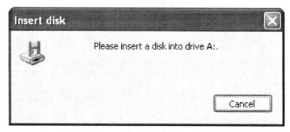

- Check that you selected the right drive and that your drive contains a storage device (such as a floppy disk, a ZIP disk or a CD-ROM).

*While you are working on your computer, a blue screen (jokingly called the "blue screen of death") suddenly appears telling you that a system error has occurred. It is not as fatal as it appears !*

## SYSTEM ERROR

▨ This message usually starts with the letters OE followed by other letters and numbers: these are memory addresses. It means that different items are occupying the same place in memory (this is called a memory conflict). To solve this problem, Windows invites you to press the keys [Ctrl] [Alt] and [Del] simultaneously. This action allows the system to restart (or to reboot).

If you made any changes to open documents without saving them to disk before this incident occurred, you will lose these changes.

*When you start an application or while you are working with it, you may see a message referring to a specific file.*

## FILE ERRORS

▨ If the message indicates an error in a file (in a .DLL file, for example), try stopping and restarting the application.

If the message indicates that Windows could not find a file that it needs to carry out an action you requested, try again. If the message appears once more, you may need to re-install the application. To ensure that you do not aggravate the problem, contact your computer store or computer hotline.

*While you are working on your computer, Windows may show a warning window after it was unable to find a file it needed.*

## CLOSE WINDOW

▨ In most cases you need only click the **Close** button: Windows will shut down the application, which you can then restart.

 In computing jargon, people speak of a system having "crashed". This means that for some (hardware or software) technical reason, the system is unable to carry out your request. There are generally not many things you can do in this case. If your computer is completely blocked, restart it. If you suspect your hardware to be the root of the problem, check your connections. Otherwise, restart your computer and your application. Very often, everything will then be alright: you may have lost only the latest changes you made to the document on which you were working at the time of the crash (the changes you made since you last saved your document to disk).

# Technical problems

 If your computer does not switch off immediately when you press the Power button, keep this button pressed in for a few seconds.

*With certain Windows applications, such as Word, you may find that when you choose a certain option, the application will show a message to tell you that it needs a certain component in order to comply with your request.*

## OFFICE APPLICATION MESSAGE

▦ A dialog box appears offering to install a new feature.

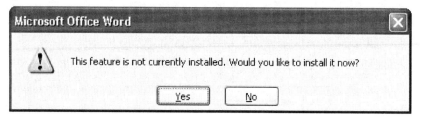

As the section on **Managing folders and files** describes, applications are often installed with only those features that are most commonly used. With this message, the application indicates that it needs a feature that is not currently installed and offers to install it for you.

▦ If you want to go ahead with your action, insert the application (or Office suite CD-ROM in this example) in your CD-ROM drive and click **Yes** or **OK**.

Windows will get the missing file(s) from the **CD-ROM** then you can carry on working.

▦ If you do not want to install this feature, click **No** or **Cancel**.

Windows will then allow you to carry on working without using this feature.

Troubleshooting

*And when the hardware gets involved...*

## HARDWARE PROBLEM

▨ A common cause of hardware problems is the cable connection.

▨ When you start up your computer, you may find that a <u>hardware item is no longer working</u> (such as your mouse, for example) even though it was working correctly the last time you used your computer. First, check all the connections: for example, you could take out and put back in each connection in turn. This simple approach alone may be enough to solve the problem.

▨ If your <u>main unit does not start</u>: are you sure it is switched on? Some central units have an on/off switch on the back panel with the connectors: is this switch in the | or **on** position? If so, check that the unit's **on** indicator is lit: if it is not lit then you may have a real problem and you must contact the computer store that supplied you with the machine.

▨ The <u>number pad does not work</u>: have you activated the Num Lock? Check the NumLock indicator: if it is not lit, press the ⌨ key to activate the Num Lock and light this indicator.

*Suppose that you must print some important documents, but your printer is leaving traces on the paper.*

## PRINTER PROBLEM

▨ If you have a laser printer, clean the corona wire on the drum. Consult your printer's user manual for this purpose. With some models, when you take out the drum you can see a mirror: it is sometimes sufficient simply to clean this mirror (above all, do not use any cleaning products for this purpose: use only a soft dry cloth).

▨ Ink jet printers may also leave traces. This problem is usually caused by dirty ink cartridges: you should be able to solve this problem by removing the ink cartridges and cleaning them. Some printers have a special head-cleaning cycle; you could use this to solve messy printing problems.

*Unexpected pages may appear when you are surfing the Web.*

## INTERNET ERRORS

▨ Two types of Internet error messages most frequently occur:

**Error 404**      indicates that a page of an existing site is not available. Click the **Back** button in your browser and test another link.

# Technical problems

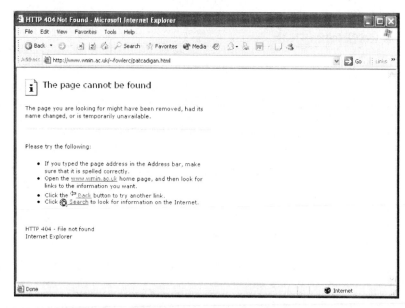

**Cannot display page** indicates that an Internet site or page is not available. Try clicking the **Back** button in your browser and repeating your action.

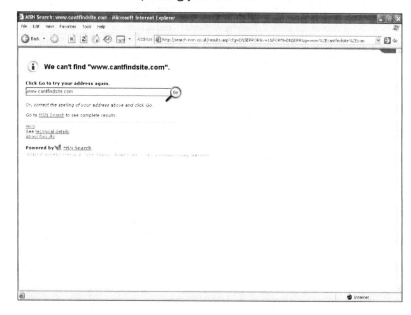

# ─Index─────────────

## A

**ADDRESS**

| | |
|---|---|
| Typical e-mail address | 162 |
| Typical web page address | 161 |

**ALIGNING**

| | |
|---|---|
| Paragraphs | 81 |

**APPLICATION**

| | |
|---|---|
| Adding extra component | 170 |
| Closes unexpectedly | 169 |
| Closing an application window | 61 |
| Closing Works applications | 106 |
| Installing | 134 |
| Starting from the start menu | 52 |
| Starting in Works | 86 |
| Starting the Word application | 64 |
| Starting your Web browser | 158 |
| Typical e-mail application | 163 |
| Uninstalling | 136 |

See also E-MAIL, INTERNET, WINDOWS
MEDIA PLAYER, WORD, WORKS

**ATTACHMENT**

| | |
|---|---|
| Attaching files to e-mail | 166 |

## B

**BRIEFCASE**

| | |
|---|---|
| Description | 138 |

| | |
|---|---|
| Using | 138 |

**BROWSER**

| | |
|---|---|
| Description | 158 |
| Displaying a Web page | 159 |
| Starting | 158 |

## C

**CALCULATION**

| | |
|---|---|
| Entering formula in cell | 95 |

**CD**

| | |
|---|---|
| Playing on the Media Player | 145 |

**CELL**

| | |
|---|---|
| Copying contents to other cells | 97 |
| Deleting contents | 95 |
| Editing contents | 94 |
| Entering formula | 95 |
| Entering function in formula | 96 |
| Formatting characters | 101 |

**CHARACTER**

| | |
|---|---|
| Formatting | 78 |
| Formatting (spreadsheet) | 101 |

**CLOSING**

| | |
|---|---|
| Application | 61 |
| Document | 77 |
| Switching off your computer | 50 |
| Windows XP session | 49 |
| Works applications | 106 |

# —Index

Works document 103

## COLUMN

Changing width 99
Deleting from spreadsheet 99
Inserting in spreadsheet 98

## COMPUTER

See HARDWARE, PORTABLE
COMPUTER, WINDOWS XP

## CONNECTING

To the Internet 154

## COPYING

Cell contents to other cells 97
Files/folders 123
Files/folders onto floppy disk 124
Text 74

## DELETING

Cell contents 95
Files/folders 124
Managing Recycle Bin contents 126
Text 71

## DESKTOP

Description of XP desktop 46

## DEVICE

Digital cameras 39

Joystick 40
Modems 36
PCMCIA cards 41
Printers 34
Scanners 38
USB flash drives 41
ZIP drive 37

## DIALOG BOX

Using 60

## DIGITAL CAMERA

Description 39

## DOCUMENT

Closing 77
Creating in Works 90
Opening 76
Printing 83
Printing in Works 104
Printing part of 83
Saving (existing) 77
Saving (new) 74
Saving under another name 76
Saving/opening/closing in Works 103
Using the Word print preview 82

See also FILE

## DRIVE

Accessing with Windows Explorer 110
CD-ROM/DVD 25
Floppy disk 24
System cannot find 168

# —Index

**DVD**

Capturing a still image      152
Playing on the Media Player      150

## E

**E-MAIL**

Elements of an address      162
Receiving mail      165
Sending a message      163
Typical e-mail application      163

**EDITING**

Spreadsheet cell contents      94

**ENTERING DATA**

Entering spreadsheet data      93
Entering text in Word      67
Filling in a dialog box      60
Using Insert/Overtype mode      69

*See also CELL, TEXT*

**ERROR**

Application component error      170
Close window error      169
File errors      169
Hardware troubleshooting      171
Inaccessible drive errors      168
Internet error messages      171
Printer troubleshooting      171
System (blue screen)      169
System disk errors      168

**EXPLORER**

*See WINDOWS EXPLORER*

**EXPLORER BAR**

Displaying      109

## F

**FILE**

Attaching to e-mail message      166
Copying      123
Copying onto floppy disk      124
Deleting      124
File errors      169
Finding by name      119
Managing in Recycle Bin      126
Moving      122
Selecting      118
Working with the Briefcase      138

*See also DOCUMENT, FOLDER*

**FILL HANDLE**

Using to copy cell contents      97

**FINDING**

*See SEARCH*

**FLOPPY DISK**

Causing system disk error      168
Copying files/folders      124
Description of disk/drive      24
Formatting      127

# —Index

**FOLDER**

Accessing with Windows Explorer    110
Copying    123
Copying onto floppy disk    124
Creating new    116
Deleting    124
Description of My Documents    108
Managing in Recycle Bin    126
Moving    122
Selecting    118
Working with the Briefcase    138

**FORMATTING**

Characters    78
Floppy disk    127

**FORMULA**

Entering function    96
Entering in spreadsheet cell    95

**FUNCTION**

Entering in formula    96

**HARD DISK**

Description    22
USB flash drives    41

**HARDWARE**

CD-ROM/DVD drive    25
Floppy drive    24
Hard disk    22

Main unit contents    13
Memory    23
Processor    21
Troubleshooting    171
Using the keyboard    26
Using the mouse    31
*See also DEVICE*

**HYPERLINK**

Activating in a Web page    160

**INSERT**

Using Insert/Overtype mode    69

**INSERTION POINT**

Moving in text    71

**INSTALLING**

Application    134
Modems    154
Printers    130
Uninstalling an application    136

**INTERNET**

Common error messages    171
Contacting a service provider    155
Description of various uses    157
Displaying a Web page    159
Installing a modem    154
Installing ISP connection kit    156

# —Index

Starting your web browser     158
What you need     154

## ISP

Contacting to subscribe     155
Installing ISP connection kit     156

## J

### JOYSTICK

Description     40

## K

### KEYBOARD

Using     26

## L

### LAYOUT

Managing several windows     55

### LOG ON/OFF

Logging off from Windows XP     49
Logging on to Windows XP     44

## M

### MAIN UNIT

Ports and connections     13
Using     20
What it contains     13

### MEMORY

Description     23

### MENU

Using menus & options     58
Using shortcut keys     58
Using the Control menu     53

### MENU OPTION

Activating     58

### MESSAGE

Attaching files     166
Receiving mail     165
Sending an e-mail message     163

### MODEM

Description     36
Installing     154

### MOUSE

Cleaning     33
Using     31

### MOVING

Files/folders     122

# —Index

Insertion point in text     71
Text     74
Window     54
Within spreadsheet     92

**MULTIMEDIA**

Using the Windows Media Player     144

**MY DOCUMENTS**

Description of contents     108

*See also WINDOWS EXPLORER*

**OPENING**

Document     76
Menus     58
Windows Media Player     144
Works document     103
Works Task Launcher     87

*See also LOG ON/OFF*

**PARAGRAPH**

Changing alignment     81

**PCMCIA CARD**

Description     41

**PORT**

Main unit ports and connections     13

**PORTABLE COMPUTER**

Description of keyboard     26
Historical overview     12
Installing second screen     133
Main hardware elements     12
Switching off     50

*See also HARDWARE, WINDOWS XP*

**PRINT PREVIEW**

Using in Word     82
Using in Works     103

**PRINTER**

Description     34
Installing     130
Troubleshooting     171

**PRINTING**

Document     83
Part of document     83
Using the Word print preview     82
Using the Works print preview     103
Works document     104

**PROCESSOR**

Description     21

**PROGRAM**

*See APPLICATION*

# ─Index────────

## R

**RADIO**

| | |
|---|---|
| Finding Internet radio stations | 148 |
| Listening to Internet radio | 148 |
| Using the Radio Tuner | 147 |

**RECEIVING**

| | |
|---|---|
| E-mail message | 165 |

**RECYCLE BIN**

| | |
|---|---|
| Managing contents | 126 |

**RESIZING**

| | |
|---|---|
| Changing spreadsheet column width | 99 |
| Changing spreadsheet row height | 100 |
| Window | 54 |

**ROW**

| | |
|---|---|
| Changing height | 100 |
| Deleting from spreadsheet | 99 |
| Inserting in spreadsheet | 98 |

## S

**SAVING**

| | |
|---|---|
| Document under another name | 76 |
| Existing document | 77 |
| New document | 74 |
| Works document | 103 |

**SCANNER**

| | |
|---|---|
| Description | 38 |

**SCREEN**

| | |
|---|---|
| Installing second screen | 133 |

**SEARCH**

| | |
|---|---|
| Finding files by name | 119 |
| Finding Internet radio stations | 148 |

**SELECTING**

| | |
|---|---|
| Files/folders | 118 |
| Text | 72 |

**SENDING**

| | |
|---|---|
| E-mail message | 163 |

**SOCKET**

*See PORT*

**SPREADSHEET**

| | |
|---|---|
| Deleting rows/columns | 99 |
| Description of Works spreadsheet | 91 |
| Entering data | 93 |
| Formatting characters | 101 |
| Inserting rows/columns | 98 |
| Moving within | 92 |
| Using the print preview | 103 |

*See also CELL, COLUMN, FORMULA, ROW*

**START MENU**

| | |
|---|---|
| Description of main features | 47 |
| Starting an application | 52 |

# — Index

**STARTING**

Application in Works 86
Microsoft Word 64
Microsoft Works 86
Web browser 158
Windows XP 44

*See also OPENING*

**SYSTEM**

Cannot find drive 168
Close window error 169
Disk error 168
File errors 169
General system errors 169

**TAB**

Inserting in text 69

**TASK**

Creating new in Works 90

**TASK LAUNCHER**

Opening 87
Using 88
Using to start an application 89

**TEXT**

Changing paragraph alignment 81
Deleting 71
Entering in Word 67
Formatting characters 78

Inserting tabs 69
Moving the insertion point 71
Moving/copying 74
Selecting 72
Using Insert/Overtype mode 69

**TOOLBAR**

*See MENU, WINDOW*

**TROUBLESHOOTING**

*See ERROR*

**USB FLASH DRIVES**

Description 41

**VIDEO**

Playing DVDs 150

**VIEW**

Changing look of Media Player 152
Changing presentation of file/
folder list 113

# —Index

## W

### WEB

| | |
|---|---|
| Description | 158 |

*See also INTERNET*

### WEB PAGE

| | |
|---|---|
| Activating hyperlinks | 160 |
| Displaying in browser | 159 |

### WINDOW

| | |
|---|---|
| Closes unexpectedly | 169 |
| Closing an application window | 61 |
| Description of main elements | 53 |
| Description of My Documents | 108 |
| Managing several open windows | 55 |
| Moving | 54 |
| Resizing | 54 |
| Using dialog boxes | 60 |
| Word application window | 65 |

*See also WINDOWS EXPLORER, WINDOWS XP, WORKSCREEN*

### WINDOWS EXPLORER

| | |
|---|---|
| Accessing drives/folders | 110 |
| Changing presentation of file/ folder list | 113 |
| Copying files/folders | 123 |
| Creating a folder | 116 |
| Deleting files/folders | 124 |
| Description of My Documents window | 108 |
| Displaying explorer bars | 109 |
| Finding files by name | 119 |
| Moving files/folders | 122 |
| Selecting files/folders | 118 |

### WINDOWS MEDIA PLAYER

| | |
|---|---|
| Changing appearance (skins) | 152 |
| Opening | 144 |
| Using to listen to the radio | 147 |
| Using to play an audio CD | 145 |
| Using to play DVDs | 150 |

### WINDOWS XP

| | |
|---|---|
| Description of desktop | 46 |
| Description of start menu | 47 |
| Logging off | 49 |
| Starting | 44 |
| Switching off your computer | 50 |

*See also WINDOWS EXPLORER*

### WORD

| | |
|---|---|
| Closing document | 77 |
| Entering text | 67 |
| Looking at the workscreen | 65 |
| Opening document | 76 |
| Saving existing document | 77 |
| Saving new document | 74 |
| Starting | 64 |

*See also TEXT*

### WORKS

| | |
|---|---|
| Closing applications | 106 |
| Creating a document | 90 |
| Description of spreadsheet | 91 |
| Opening the Task Launcher | 87 |
| Saving/opening/closing documents | 103 |
| Starting | 86 |

# —Index

Starting an application      86

Starting an application from
the Task Launcher      89

Using the Task Launcher      88

*See also SPREADSHEET*

**WORKSCREEN**

Description of Works spreadsheet      91

Windows XP desktop      46

Word application window      65

## Z

**ZIP DRIVE**

Description      37